NATURAL HIGHS

A Guide to Outdoor Activities

NATURAL HIGHS

A Guide to Outdoor Activities

Steve Short and Bernie Palmer

Whitecap Books
Vancouver / Toronto

Edited by Bruce Obee
Cover and interior photographs by Steve Short
Cover and interior design by Carolyn Deby

Typeset by CompuType, Vancouver, B.C.

Printed and bound in Canada by D.W. Friesen and Sons Ltd.

Canadian Cataloguing in Publication Data

Short, Steve.
  Natural highs

  Includes index.
  ISBN 1-55110-021-5

  1. Natural history — British Columbia — Guide-books
2.British Columbia — Description and travel — 1981 —
Guide-books. I. Title.
QH106.2.B7S56 1992   508.711   C92-091017-3

Disclaimer
The author, editor, and publisher of *Best of B.C. Natural Highs*
have used their best efforts to inform the reader as to the
risks inherent in the outdoor activities described in this book.
The level of expertise required to travel into largely unmarked,
remote, and hazardous areas must be decided by the reader.
Safety is the responsibility of the individual. If there is any
doubt, please consult a guide who is familiar with the area to
be explored. We take no responsibility for any loss or injury
incurred by anyone using information contained in this book.

To our parents with love.

Stone sheep near Muncho Lake.

Table of Contents

Thanks to . . .

The staff of various government ministries, both federal and provincial, in Parks, Tourism, Forestry, Environment, and the numerous outdoor recreation organizations. Jack Apps for sharing his rafting experience down the Tatshenshini River. Gail Ross for her enthusiasm and suggestions for selecting highlights. Ian Pepper and John Penner for their generosity with transportation to coastal highlights. John Youds for his insight regarding white pelicans. Kent Sedgwick, president of the Mackenzie Trail Association, for his time and energy in providing details.

Our warmest, heartfelt thanks to our fathers, Fergie Short and Dwayne Palmer. Fergie for his perseverance and dedication as travel companion, and fact recorder. Dwayne for his outdoor ethics, vast knowledge of Peace River-Alaska Highway and for being our bush pilot into remote areas.

Special appreciation to our editor Bruce Obee for his patience, wisdom, kindness, and humour. Sincere thanks to Carolyn Deby for her creative talents in design, and our publisher Colleen MacMillan for her faith and encouragement.

Kinuseo Falls in Monkman Park.

The Best Of British Columbia

There are many reasons we consider certain places the most beautiful, most spectacular, the best. The alpenglow on a mountain top, the season, the companions, or the mood of the moment. "Best," like beauty, is in the eye of the beholder and in B.C. there's a great deal to behold. So we loaded the jeep with film, granola bars, and outdoors paraphernalia and set off in search of places we could call the "Best of B.C."

With help from parks and forestry officials, local residents, and outdoor enthusiasts we chose our highlights for a variety of reasons. Mount Robson for its size, Emerald Lake for its beauty, the Pocket Desert for its rarity, the Carmanah Valley for its endangered status, Idaho Peak as a personal preference. In all, we found more than a hundred natural highlights which we consider to be B.C.'s best. Many are simple roadside stops; others are day hikes or short canoe journeys. Some are long, uphill backpacking ordeals, where we battled mosquitos and slogged through rain-ridden trails. Some of the most isolated are fly-in or horseback destinations.

Initially reluctant to share our discoveries, we agreed that by highlighting the natural features of B.C. we could improve public awareness, encouraging the preservation of these special places. There is so much here to cherish, yet so little protected.

The wilderness of B.C. is an invitation for anyone to explore, to discover, and to appreciate the importance of keeping it intact. Our book provides a glimpse of B.C.'s best. Enjoy the adventure of finding these natural highlights yourself. We did, and found many surprises, inspiration, and indelible memories.

Steve Short and Bernie Palmer — Burnaby, B.C., January, 1992

Brandywine Falls near Whistler.

British Columbia

B.C.'s scenic diversity is admired by outback travellers from around the world. Mountains and glaciers, fiords and dormant volcanoes, ancient forests and deserted beaches. The continent's wildest river, Canada's only desert, and the nation's highest waterfall are found here. There are more than 6,000 lakes, 11,000 rivers and streams, and a multitude of soothing hot springs. From the mild, Mediterranean climate of the coast to the near-arctic conditions of the north, B.C. is a province of constantly changing landscapes.

Predominantly mountainous terrain, with more than sixty ranges, numerous valleys, extensive plateaus and plains make up B.C. Running north to south, the major mountain ranges vanish at the edge of the sea, only to reappear as the Queen Charlotte Islands and Vancouver Island. The Coast Mountains are the highest in North America. Fairweather Mountain, in the extreme northwest corner, at 4,663 metres is the highest point in B.C. The central and southern regions feature a series of plateaus and mountain ranges, such as the Stikine, Skeena, Cascade, Monashee, Purcell, Selkirk, and Columbia mountains. These are set apart from the Rockies, by the Rocky Mountain Trench, a fault extending from the United States border to the northern reaches of the province.

Natural Highlight Regions of B.C.

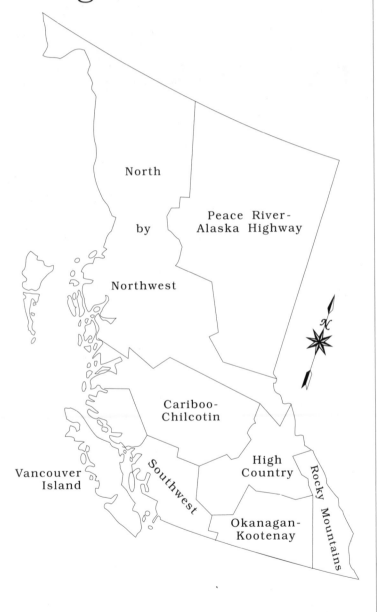

North

by

Peace River-
Alaska Highway

Northwest

Cariboo-
Chilcotin

High
Country

Rocky Mountains

Southwest

Vancouver
Island

Okanagan-
Kootenay

Location and Access

British Columbia, encompassing 948,600 square kilometres is Canada's third largest province. It is surrounded by scenic areas, with Alaska to the northwest, the Yukon and the Northwest Territories to the north, Alberta to the east, Washington, Idaho and Montana states bordering the south and 27,200 kilometres of convoluted Pacific coastline to the west. International airlines link B.C. to more than forty countries, and provincial and local charter airlines serve communities within the province. B.C. Ferries from the mainland sail to Vancouver Island, the Gulf Islands, and the Queen Charlotte Islands. They also run the famous Inside Passage route from northern Vancouver Island to Prince Rupert. Visitors coming from the U.S. can travel by ferry from either Washington or Alaska. Contact B.C. Ferries or Travel Infocentres for schedules and reservations.

Main road access to B.C. is via the Trans-Canada Highway (Highway 1) from the Prairies and central Canada or the Yellowhead Highway (Highway 5) from Edmonton, Alberta. Interstate 5 leads north from Washington State, the Alaska Highway south from the Yukon. There are sixteen points of entry for motorists travelling from the U.S. border into B.C.

To ensure a good trip to B.C., plan ahead by acquiring topographical maps and specific guide books for the region in which you're interested. Up-to-date road maps are available from Infocentres. A variety of maps, including administrative boundary maps, provincial park maps and various scales of the National Topographic Series maps for all areas of the province may be purchased from the Geological Survey of Canada sales office in Vancouver. In smaller towns the office of the Government Agent usually has a small supply of topographical maps for sale. Outdoor recreation maps, indicating the areas used for all types of outdoor recreation, are also available. For information on road conditions call the Ministry of Transportation and Highways Infoline for a twenty-four hour recorded message giving up to date reports.

Highlights reached by logging roads require care: huge trucks rule the road and travel at great speeds. On back-country roads there are no services: ensure you have a full tank of gas, spare tire, repair tools, and plenty of windshield washer fluid.

Always inform others of your travel plans. B.C. has a Tourist Alert system. If your name appears in a newspaper, at an Infocentre, or is broadcast on radio or television, contact the nearest police department.

Information Services and Tips

The Best of B.C. Natural Highs is not designed to give lessons in wilderness survival. We assume the reader venturing into the wilderness already has basic outdoor skills. On any outing beyond a short walk a basic survival kit should be carried. The farther you are from help the more caution should be exercised. Leave your dog at home, not only for consideration of the area and other travellers but for your safety as well: dogs have been known to attract bears and in some cases lead them right back to you.

Wheelchair travellers can obtain information about travelling in the province by contacting the Canadian Paraplegic Association. Services for hearing impaired are available at the Western Institute for the Deaf. All addresses are located in the back of the book.

More than 140 communities throughout B.C. are members of the Travel Infocentre network. They operate centres providing tourist information about their area and the entire province. Most infocentres are conspicuous and some are staffed by certified travel counsellors. They can help reserve accommodation or book tours. Not all communities have infocentres, depending on the enthusiasm of the local

Snow geese at George C. Reifel Migratory Bird Sanctuary.

chamber of commerce. Chambers of commerce are usually listed in phone directories. Contact addresses for the regional tourist offices are listed in the back of this book.

Accommodations and Camping

You'll find accommodations to suit every traveller in B.C. Resort lodges, hotels, motels, family inns, bed and breakfast, hostels, and campgrounds range from deluxe to primitive. Things get crowded in summer and on holidays so book well ahead. Tourism B.C.'s *Accommodations* guide, available free from Travel Infocentres throughout B.C., or by writing to Tourism B.C., is the best source for annually updated information listing locations, phone numbers and prices.

There are 11,000 campsites in about 150 provincial parks. Campgrounds range in services, from basic facilities with flush or pit toilets, fireplaces, picnic tables, wood supply and water to some with showers and shelters or lodges. There are nightly fees and reservations are not taken for provin-

Pristine lakes and alpine tundra in the Rainbow Range.

cial or national park campgrounds so select your site early in the day. Many parks offer discounts or free camping for seniors and handicapped people. A few campgrounds have group campsites for which reservations are required.

In B.C. it is legal to camp on Crown land as long as you aren't violating any permit or lease, and no special restrictions or fire closures are in effect. Off-the-beaten track campsites, some set aside by B.C. Forest Service or forest companies, are scattered throughout the bush, usually adjacent to logging roads. In some outback areas of provincial parks, wilderness camping is allowed but open fires are prohibited. Anyone is welcome to use these sites and simple respect for those who follow is expected.

Fire is a serious threat throughout B.C. in summer. Ensure that campfires are completely extinguished before going to bed or leaving a campsite for any period of time. In case of fire dial "0" and ask for Zenith 5555.

Parks

B.C. has five national parks — Yoho, Kootenay, Glacier, Mount Revelstoke, and Pacific Rim. Negotiations for a sixth park known as Gwaii Haanas-South Moresby, on the Queen Charlotte Islands, were under way as this book went to press. Except at Pacific Rim Park, on Vancouver Island, permits, available from park headquarters, are required to tour Canadian national parks.

Nearly four hundred provincial parks including over thirty coastal marine parks, recreation areas, and wilderness conservancies, are managed by the provincial government through BC Parks. Most are protected areas intended for recreational use only.

Recreation areas are tracts of land that will eventually become parks but currently may be used for industrial purposes. Wilderness and nature conservancies are roadless tracts where natural ecological communities are preserved. No development of any kind is permitted. An ecological reserve is Crown land, or sometimes donated or leased private land, where the natural ecosystem is preserved for scientific study and educational use. More than 130 ecological reserves in B.C. cover over 157,000 hectares, approximately one-third of them in marine waters.

The provincial government is planning parks to protect examples of fifty-nine distinctive landscapes found within B.C.

Climate, Flora and Fauna

B.C.'s diverse terrain and climate cause tremendous variation in wildlife habitats and vegetation. Mountains and stretches of water separate the regions, ensuring a variety that includes all but tropical and polar climates. Trees dominate the landscape of more than half of B.C., with rainfall and climate determining the distribution of the various species. In addition to conifers, over two thousand species of flowering plants are found within B.C.

On the coast, with more than three hundred centimetres of annual rain, winters are wet and mild, summers are moderate. Lush rain forests of western red cedar, hemlock, Sitka spruce, and Douglas fir here are thickly carpeted with ferns and shrubs.

Weather watchers are intrigued by statistics from the southern interior of B.C. The Okanagan has two thousand hours of sunshine a year; Ashcroft has the lowest precipitation with fifteen centimetres a year. Canada's only true desert, with cacti and rattlesnakes, is found in this area, and Lillooet holds the province's record as the hottest spot — 44 degrees Celsius.

The climate farther east in the Kootenays is moderate with summer temperatures in the mid-thirties. This is a land of scrub, ponderosa pine, sagebrush, mountain hemlock, subalpine fir, Englemann spruce, and Douglas fir.

Farther north, in the Cariboo, are stands of lodgepole pine and spruce, interspersed with deciduous trembling aspen. In most northerly reaches of the province, summers are short and dry, winters are long and chilled by cold Arctic air. Large trees up here give way to more stunted species — willow, birch, and white and black spruce. Above the forests lie alpine krummholz, twisted shrubs, delicate wildflowers, grasses, and lichens.

With such climatic diversity outdoors travellers in B.C. should be prepared for anything from frostbite to heat stroke. Weather can change without much warning: make sure you can protect yourself from the sun, wind, rain, and cold. In summer carry sunscreen, particularly on the water, as well as insect repellent for ticks, mosquitos, and other bugs. Ticks are a nuisance where large animals live: if you are bitten, remove the whole creature.

More than a million birds use the Pacific flyway migration routes. Countless waterfowl, swans, geese and ducks, inhabit the wetlands. Although B.C. boasts the highest density of red-throated loons in the world, three species, including the western grebe, American white pelican, and spotted owl, have virtually run out of nesting habitats, and many more are endangered, threatened or of special concern.

B.C. has populations of killer whales (orcas), Pacific grays, minkes, and humpback whales. Harbour seals, dolphins, sea otters, and sea lions thrive off the coast. Five species of salmon travel Pacific waters and shellfish proliferate along the coastline. Inland lakes and streams contain seventy-two fish species.

Twenty-five percent of the world's grizzly bears, in addition to a large population of black bears, inhabit B.C. The most fearful of animals likely to be encountered, especially in wilderness areas, are bears. They rarely eat people, but bears can attack when startled, especially if they are feeding or resting with cubs. People cause conflicts with bears by approaching them too closely, offering them food, attempting to drive them off, or trying to save apparently orphaned cubs. If you see a bear at a distance, detour around it or wait until it leaves the area before continuing your journey. Avoid making the animal feel threatened — always leave an escape route. If you encounter a bear at close quarters,

Kayaking through Skookumchuck Narrows is only for experts.

slowly back away while talking to it calmly. This sometimes can alleviate any sense of threat to the bear, and may help you not to panic. Backing away allows you to watch for aggressive behavior; snapping of jaws, making a woofing sound, or lowering its head with the ears pinned back. If there's a climbable tree slowly move toward it and climb as high as possible. Most adult grizzlies cannot climb trees but young grizzlies and black bears can. If you are attacked by a black bear, playing dead seldom works. As a last resort try intimidating the bear by making noise or swinging large sticks. If attacked by a grizzly, curling up protecting your face, neck and stomach sometimes works. Leave your pack on for protection. Don't move until you are sure the bear has gone, even if he cuffs you a bit. With grizzlies, fighting back usually makes them mad, but as they're unpredictable, it could persuade one to leave you alone.

If you are travelling in bear country you may wish to consider carrying bear bangers, or chemical repellants. Information on where to obtain these should be available at large outfitting stores.

Avoid bears by staying away from areas they are likely to be: they frequent alpine areas early in summer, feeding on marmots and fresh shoots of plants. Later in the season they're found near berries. During salmon runs they inhabit river valleys. Use a flashlight at night when camping and hang food in trees, well away from the campsite, don't cook in or near your tent, and don't leave garbage around. BC Park rangers monitor grizzly areas for potential danger and post warning signs. Other inhabitants of B.C. include cougars, lynx, wolverines, wolves, bighorn, Dall and Stone sheep, goats, and several species of deer including moose, caribou, and elk. The small creatures include hoary marmots, porcupines, beavers, chipmunks, badgers, pikas, and snakes.

There are rattlesnakes in Okanagan-Kootenay, especially in the Osoyoos area and around Vaseux Lake. If you watch where you step and avoid putting hands in rock crevices you should have no problems. If you get bitten, don't make an incision but apply a pressure dressing above the puncture, immobilize the limb and keep it below the level of the heart; then get medical attention quickly.

Here is a simple table to help you understand the metric system:

WHEN YOU KNOW	MULTIPLY BY	TO FIND
centimetres	.4	inches
metres	3.3	feet
kilometres	.63	miles
square metres	1.25	square yards
square kilometres	.4	square miles
hectares	2.5	acres
kilograms	2.2	pounds

OR:

inches	2.5	centimetres
feet	.3	metres
miles	1.6	kilometres
square yards	.8	square metres
square miles	2.6	square kilometres
acres	.4	hectares
pounds	.45	kilograms

FAHRENHEIT/ CELSIUS

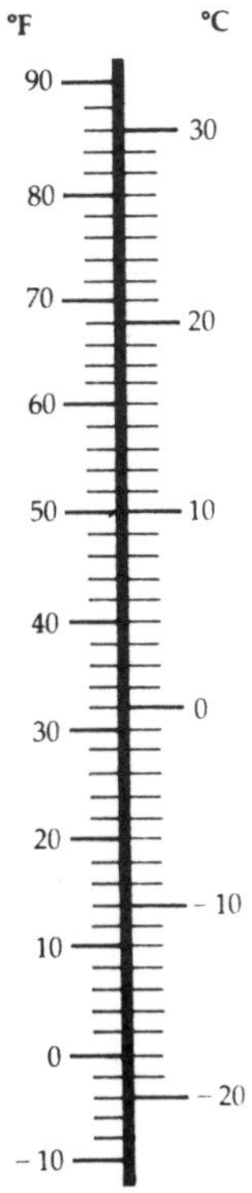

Temperatures are given in Celsius and their relationship to the Fahrenheit scale is shown at right.

Sitka spruce in Carmanah Valley.

Vancouver Island

Vancouver Island, 450 kilometres long, encompasses 32,137 square kilometres. The largest North American island in the Pacific, it lies in the southwest corner of B.C., separated from the mainland by Queen Charlotte, Georgia, and Juan de Fuca straits.

Aside from 3,440 kilometres of intricate coastline, the island's major feature is a central spine of mountains running its entire length. Vancouver Island Ranges rise to 2,200 metres, separating the west coast from the eastern lowlands, causing a dramatic effect on the climate. Weather systems approaching from the west slam into the mountain barrier. Forced to rise over the terrain, they release moisture on the west side of the mountains, making the area one of the wettest places on the continent. Annual rainfall for some locations exceeds three hundred centimetres. The region east of the mountains in the rainshadow is drier, to the extent that cactus can be found on some Gulf Islands.

Variations in terrain and weather result in a great diversity of natural attractions — long stretches of deserted sandy beach, clusters of offshore evergreen islands, luxuriant rain forests with Canada's largest trees. Some of the coastal scenery can be viewed along the West Coast Trail, one of Canada's most famous hiking routes. In the mountains, where steep terrain and glaciers combine to irrigate fields of alpine flowers, there are innumerable waterfalls including Della Falls, Canada's highest. Off the east coast are the sheltered waterways of the Gulf Islands as well as some of

Vancouver Island

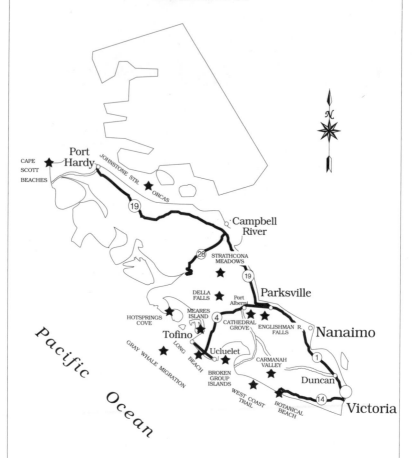

CAPE SCOTT BEACHES ★
Port Hardy ★
JOHNSTONE STR.
ORCAS ★
19
Campbell River
28
STRATHCONA MEADOWS ★
19
DELLA FALLS ★
Port Alberni
Parksville
HOTSPRINGS COVE
MEARES ISLAND ★
4
CATHEDRAL GROVE ★ ★
ENGLISHMAN R. FALLS
Nanaimo
Tofino ★
GRAY WHALE MIGRATION ★
LONG BEACH
Ucluelet
BROKEN GROUP ISLANDS ★
CARMANAH VALLEY ★
1
Duncan
WEST COAST TRAIL
BOTANICAL BEACH ★
14
Victoria

Pacific Ocean

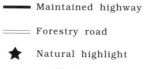

──────── Maintained highway

═══════ Forestry road

★ Natural highlight

Kilometres
25   0   25   50   75   100

0   30
Miles

Vancouver

the world's most reliable orca-watching territory. These natural highlights, and many others, attract hundreds of thousands of visitors each year. Most arrive on ferries from mainland B.C. or Washington state. Once on the island, travel is easy with a major highway running the island's length from Victoria north to Port Hardy. Other major highways lead to several scenic places, and a vast network of logging roads reaches much of the island's outback. Car rentals, bus, and air connections to communities throughout the island and mainland are available. From Victoria there is scheduled airline service to the U.S., and ferries to Washington state or mainland B.C. All of this chapter's natural highlights (or embarkation points to them) can be reached from Victoria in less than a day's drive.

On the extreme outer coast is Pacific Rim National Park featuring three distinct units, all special enough to be highlights in this book. In the mid-central mountainous area of the island lies B.C.'s oldest park, Strathcona Provincial Park, established in 1911, known for flower meadows and Della Falls. At the extreme northwest tip of the island is Cape Scott Provincial Park, featuring wild beaches inaccessible to automobiles but available to day hikers and backpackers. Dozens of other provincial parks are found throughout the island, many offering excellent campsites, others catering to picnickers and beach lovers.

Exploring the island requires proper dress. The operative word here is rain, especially on the west coast. But with good boots and rain gear, wet weather need not be a deterrent to enjoying the outdoors. For short day hikes along beaches, poking around tidepools, and through boggy forests, rubber boots are probably better than hiking boots. Sturdier footwear, well proven before the trip, is necessary for trips like the West Coast Trail or ventures into the mountains. We have taken to carrying an umbrella even on backpacking trips to contend with drizzle or brief squalls where wind isn't a factor. An umbrella eliminates the need to stop, remove packs, don rain gear, and get going again, often just in time for the sun to break through. Whatever system of clothing and equipment you prefer, staying dry is a challenge and a necessity, especially on overnight trips where it may not be possible to get a fire going to dry out soggy clothing.

Natural hazards are no greater than anywhere else in B.C. but visitors should be aware of a few. There are no grizzly bears or rattlesnakes on Vancouver Island. There are large numbers of black bears, however. Cougar, which are rarely seen, occasionally try to seize small children. There is far more danger from the ocean than from bears or cougars. People routinely underestimate the danger of ocean waves. The rule of thumb is to "never turn your back on the sea." Waves pounding the shoreline are not all the same size. Usually waves occur in sets of seven-to-ten "regular size" waves followed by a couple of much bigger ones and occasionally, a freak monster wave. Unwary tidepool-pokers have been caught by surprise by these big waves and swept away or smashed against the rocks. A teenager from England was swept off a rock at Long Beach in 1991, never to be seen again.

Wildlife viewing on the island is good. Black bears are sometimes seen in spring. Other large land mammals include elk, deer, wolves, beavers, river otters, the endangered Vancouver Island marmot, and the ubiquitous raccoon. The real star attractions on Vancouver Island are the marine mammals. The most dramatic of all island wildlife is the killer whale, or orca, found so dependably in the waters off northeast Vancouver Island in summer. Each spring upwards of twenty-one thousand Pacific gray whales pass close to shore on their migration from Baja to Alaska. Thousands of onlookers flock to the coast from March to May to witness this spectacle, easily viewed from shore or from tour boats. Sea lions, seals, and sea otters are found along the outer coast.

In addition to the mammals, the island is known for rich birdlife, being on the Pacific flyway. Over a million birds travel through during spring and fall migrations. Seabirds bob in the ocean swells, and nest on offshore islets. Bald eagles patrol the beaches, and tiny rufous hummingbirds buzz about in salmonberry thickets. In Pacific Rim National Park alone over 240 species have been recorded.

Vancouver Island has appealing natural highlights for long distance backpackers, sea kayakers and canoeists, day hikers, naturalists, and motorists. Many are perfect destinations for weekend trips. To see the ones featured in this book easily requires a busy couple of months.

BOTANICAL BEACH TIDE POOLS

• **Feature:** Best tide pools on B.C. coast • **Usual Access:** Day hike • **Time Required:** Full day from Victoria • **Nearest Highway:** Highway 4 • **Best Time To Visit:** Year round • **Maps:** NTS 1:50,000 92C/09

THE TIDE POOLS at Botanical Beach Provincial Park established in 1989, near Port Renfrew on the southwest coast of Vancouver Island, are said to be the best on the B.C. coast. Rock shelves exposed at low tides teem with marine life — starfish, sea urchins, anemones, nudibranchs, sculpins, and more. For decades these pools have attracted scientists and the area is perfect for introducing children to the fascinating world of marine biology. While most pools hold a plethora of colourful marine life, a few larger pools are barren, excellent swimming holes on hot summer days.

A hike to Botanical Beach begins at the community of Port Renfrew, about a hundred kilometres from Victoria on Highway 14, known locally as the West Coast Road. At the main intersection in Port Renfrew keep to the left and follow signs to a rough, 3.5 kilometre route to the beach. It's easier on your car, and your nerves, to hike this road.

Winter sunsets here are spectacular, reflecting the rich

Botanical Beach tide pools.

hues of the evening sky in calm waters of exposed pools. In clear weather, peaks of Washington's Olympic Mountains stand in the south, against the foaming breakers of the foreground. Photographers and artists alike are drawn to Botanical Beach's visual magic.

This area should be explored at low tides, preferably lower than two metres. Tides are listed each day in Victoria's daily newspaper. Keep an eye on tides while on the beach: people have been trapped on the wrong side of surge channels by incoming tides. People also have been swept off the rocks by pounding surf. Good rubber or hiking boots will help keep a grip on slippery, seaweed-covered rocks. Illustrated guides to intertidal life can enhance a trip to Botanical. Eagles and seabirds inhabit these shores and killer whales and gray whales occasionally pass by: bring binoculars.

Unfortunately, since the area was designated a park visitors have plundered the natural life. Ignorant visitors, like wildflower pickers of the mountain meadows, feel it's their right to take home souvenirs which invariably die. This natural area should be treated like a fine crystal shop — look but don't touch.

ACTIVE PASS

• **Feature:** Marine wildlife • **Usual Access:** Boat, ferry, or short walk on Gulf Island • **Time Required:** Day trip from Vancouver or Victoria • **Nearest Highway:** Highway 17 or Highway 99 • **Best Time To Visit:** Fall through spring

ACTIVE PASS, the busiest channel in the Gulf Islands, is a narrow passage between Galiano and Mayne islands. Well known to naturalists as a superb wildlife-viewing area, fishy waters support thousands of marine birds and mammals, often conveniently observable from the B.C. Ferries running between Tsawwassen and Swartz Bay. A small dark goose, the black brant, winters here in the thousands along with Pacific loons and western grebes. Oldsquaw ducks, rarely seen outside of the arctic by landlubber birders, migrate through the pass en-route to their northern nesting grounds. When herring are spawning in spring scores of eagles cruise the skies above the pass. Larger sea mammals such as seals, sea lions, and occasionally orcas are not uncommon visitors to Active Pass.

Ferry passengers get only a glimpse of the pass: people who want a more prolonged and relaxed view can perch on Galiano Bluffs Park and other viewpoints on Galiano Island. Looking down from high points, it's especially enjoyable to watch pigeon guillemots, a black seabird with red feet, swimming beneath the clear water in spring before runoff clouds the water.

For campers, Montague Harbour Provincial Marine Park eight kilometres from the ferry terminal at Sturdies Bay on Galiano is a popular vacation spot known for its beaches and good swimming. There are two campsites; one designated for boaters, hikers, and cyclists, the other for those with vehicles.

ENGLISHMAN RIVER FALLS

• **Feature:** Waterfalls • **Usual Access:** Day hikes • **Time Required:** Day trip • **Nearest Highway:** Highway 4 • **Best Time To Visit:** May to October

ENGLISHMAN RIVER FALLS make a pleasant day outing from Parksville. There are two sets of spectacular waterfalls and short hiking trails that form a loop through old forests with huge cedars, firs, and a profusion of ferns.

An eight-kilometre road to the falls turns off of Highway 4, thirteen kilometres west of Parksville.

A popular weekend camping spot, the falls are within Englishman River Falls Provincial Park which has a campground with 105 sites.

These falls were named after an Englishman drowned in the river, so take the hint and be careful near the edge of the precipice.

CATHEDRAL GROVE

• **Feature:** Giant Douglas firs • **Usual Access:** Roadside, easy walks • **Time Required:** Half day from Nanaimo • **Nearest Highway:** Highway 4 • **Best Time To Visit:** May to October

THIS STAND of huge Douglas firs in Macmillan Provincial Park makes a pleasant shady stop on the highway between Parksville and Port Alberni. Some of these giants are over seventy metres tall and eight hundred years old. Their thick bark weathered a forest fire that swept through the area 350 years ago.

Natural defenses could not combat the new threat of destruction at the hands of man, however. Though Macmillan Provincial Park protects the grove, the park is only 136 hectares; a tiny sample of what environmentalists have tried to save. Virtually all of the island's old-growth Douglas fir has disappeared: when completely gone, natural stands such as this never will appear again. Replanted forests elsewhere on the island will be cut again within two hundred years.

Highway 4 runs through Cathedral Grove, thirty-one kilometres west of Parksville. Wide, level, loop trails wind through the forest on both sides of the road. The biggest trees are on the south side of the highway. Some paths run past part of Cameron Lake and Cameron River. Some trails near the perimeter of the grove offer views of extensively logged areas next to the park, good places to ponder the alternatives in the debate over forest preservation.

CARMANAH VALLEY

• **Feature:** Canada's tallest spruce trees • **Usual Access:** Day hike • **Time Required:** Long day from Duncan • **Nearest Highway:** Highway 4 • **Best Time To Visit:** May to October • **Maps:** Carmanah Pacific Provincial Park brochure; Western Canada Wilderness Committee - Carmanah Valley Trail Guide

THE CARMANAH VALLEY, on southwest Vancouver Island, is home to the tallest spruce trees in Canada. Until a tree known as the Carmanah Giant was discovered in 1989, few people had ever heard of Carmanah. But with the discovery of the giant, a huge controversy to rescue the valley from loggers erupted. Environmental groups built trails into the valley and set up a research station to help the public see and learn about this incredible rain forest. Logging companies lobbied the government and launched a campaign to protect jobs they said would be lost if they couldn't log the valley. The provincial government settled the issue by protecting half the valley in a new park, leaving the upper half to the woodman's axe. Now the lower Carmanah, including the ninety-five-metre Carmanah Giant, lies within the 3,592-hectare Carmanah Pacific Provincial Park established in 1990.

Much of the park can be explored in an extremely long day from the cities of southern Vancouver Island. Along the route there are campsites at Gordon Bay Provincial Park, on the southwest side of Cowichan Lake, as well as several others around both shores of the lake. There are other campsites closer to Carmanah at Nitinat Lake. Camping is permitted in Carmanah Pacific, but is discouraged because of potential damage to the fragile ecosystem.

Ironically, those who love the valley most are its greatest threat. The area around the Carmanah Giant has been closed due to concern that footsteps of tree lovers have damaged shallow root systems. Other parts of the valley are equally appealing, however: there are trails to interesting features such as "the triplets" and other groves of giant spruce.

To reach Carmanah turn west off Highway 1 onto Highway 18 at a traffic light about five kilometres north of Duncan. About thirty kilometres from Highway 1, Highway 18 splits and you can travel along either side of Cowichan Lake. More than half of the forty-kilometre drive along the lake shores is on gravel road, which must be shared with loaded logging trucks. At the end of the lake turn west onto the Nitinat Main logging road, which joins the South Main from Franklin River after about nineteen kilometres. Don't cross the Nitinat River bridge near this junction: go left onto the Carmanah Main. This point is reached from Port Alberni via the Bamfield Road through Franklin River.

To reach the mid-Carmanah Valley (and the most exceptional spruce groves) follow the Carmanah Main for about nine kilometres from the Nitinat junction to Caycuse River bridge. Cross the bridge and turn right onto the Rosander Main. This road climbs steeply through switchbacks above Nitinat Lake for about twenty-nine kilometres to the Carmanah trail head, where you can park and camp.

Maps are available from BC Parks or the Western Canada Wilderness Committee.

BROKEN GROUP ISLANDS

• **Feature:** Archipelago • **Usual Access:** Canoes, kayaks, tours available • **Time Required:** Three to ten days • **Nearest Highway:** Highway 4 • **Best Time To Visit:** May to October • **Maps:** NTS 1:50,000 92F/04 • **Charts:** 3638 The Broken Group (Barkley Sound) 1:18,200; 3671 Barkley Sound 1:40,000

THE BROKEN GROUP ISLANDS are a cluster of a hundred-odd islands and islets covering more than a hundred square kilometres in Barkley Sound, off the southwest coast of Vancouver Island. It features protected waters for ocean kayakers and canoeists with opportunities to see marine mammals and seabirds, secluded beaches, and classic west-coast seascapes. The islands comprise one of three major areas within Pacific Rim National Park. They are extremely popular, especially during summer. It is still possible, however, to find solitude on a secluded beach during short day trips from base camps or during the off season.

One method of getting to the Broken Group is to drive Highway 4 from Port Alberni for eighty-eight kilometres, then turn south on a logging road to Toquart Bay. Toquart Bay can be a bit of a mob scene in summer, with campers and scores of boaters' vehicles parked on the beach. Vandals can be a problem here.

To avoid Toquart Bay many paddlers come by boat from

Port Alberni. The M.V. *Lady Rose* transports kayaks, canoes, and passengers to a float at Gibralter Island. The trip takes three hours and is well worth the cost for the advantages it offers. Vehicles left in Port Alberni are more secure than at Toquart Bay, and the *Lady Rose* trip eliminates the eight-kilometre paddle from Toquart Bay to the Broken Group. Schedules and fare information for the *Lady Rose*, operated by Alberni Marine Transportation company, are available from Travel Infocentres.

Because of the high use of the area, camping is restricted to eight designated sites on seven islands — Benson, Clarke, Hand, Gibralter, Gilbert, Turret, and Willis. These are well situated for easy day trips to other islands. From these camps paddlers can make excursions to see nesting seabirds, sea lions, seals, and perhaps whales.

Fires are allowed at campsites and on other beaches below the tideline but only driftwood, which is scarce, may be used. Pack a stove. Fresh water is available but of poor quality. Try and carry your own supply.

A compass and hydrographic chart are needed to navigate the intricate network of channels. Even novice paddlers can explore the less exposed eastern areas of the group as the waters are often calm and crossings between islands are short. Exposed western areas at the outer fringes of the group are subject to ocean swell and large waves. Novices should stick to the more sheltered areas. Wind is a hazard at any time of year.

The area is so popular, especially during summer, that a growing number of people are visiting during the off season to avoid crowds, despite the less enjoyable weather. June to September is the peak period but there's often good weather in May and October.

View from Michigan Creek on the West Coast Trail.

WEST COAST TRAIL

• **Feature:** World renowned coastline trail • **Usual Access:** Backpack • **Time Required:** Five to ten days • **Nearest Highway:** Highways 4 and 14 • **Best Time To Visit:** May to October • **Maps:** NTS 1:50,000 92C/09, 92C/10, 92C/11, 92C/13, 92C/14; Ministry of Crown Lands - WEST COAST TRAIL

PACIFIC RIM NATIONAL PARK'S West Coast Trail is one of the best known multiday hiking trails in North America. Originally built to help shipwrecked sailors make their way back to civilization, it now is a recreation route for backpackers from all over the world.

Running from Pachena Bay, near the village of Bamfield, to Port Renfrew on the southwest coast of Vancouver Island, much of the seventy-seven-kilometre trail runs along sand and gravel beaches and rocky shelves within sight and sound of the pounding Pacific surf. Sections not right on the beach are often just barely inland, traversing the rich greenery of

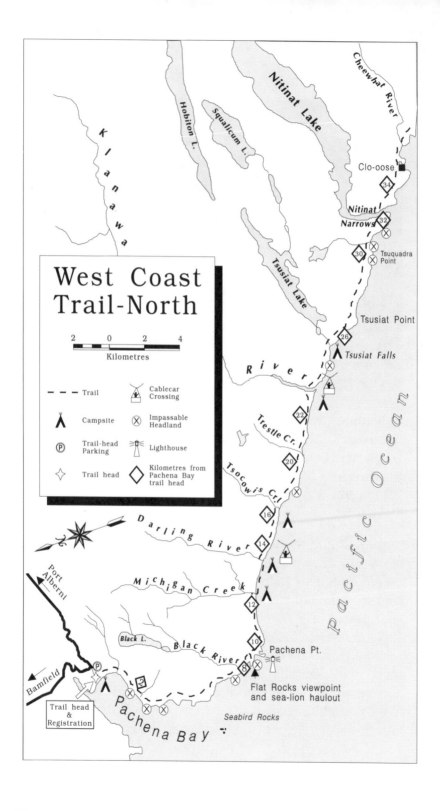

West Coast Trail-North

2 0 2 4
Kilometres

- - - Trail

🏕 Campsite

Ⓟ Trail-head Parking

✧ Trail head

🚡 Cablecar Crossing

⊗ Impassable Headland

🏮 Lighthouse

◇ Kilometres from Pachena Bay trail head

Klanawa

Hobiton L.

Squalicum L.

Nitinat Lake

Cheewhat River

Clo-oose

34

Nitinat Narrows

32

30

Tsuquadra Point

Tsusiat Lake

Tsusiat Point

26

Tsusiat Falls

River

22

Trestle Cr.

20

Tsocowis Cr.

16

14

Darling River

Michigan Creek

12

Port Alberni

10

Pachena Pt.

Bamfield

Black L.

Black River

8

Flat Rocks viewpoint and sea-lion haulout

Ⓟ

3

Trail head & Registration

Pachena Bay

Seabird Rocks

Pacific Ocean

the coastal rain forest with its massive trees, lush mosses and salal thickets.

The route, which runs generally north-south, can be hiked from either end. All groups must register with Canadian Parks Service offices in Pachena Bay or Port Renfrew. In 1992 a new reservation system for the trail was implemented, restricting the number of hikers starting from each end to twenty-six a day. It is recommended that all hikers make reservations in advance. Arriving at the trail head without a booking will mean being put on a waiting list for the next available space. This could result in a wait of several days during the peak period in summer. Reservations may be made after March 1. The first ten places must be booked in advance, while the remaining sixteen are first-come-first served. From spring to fall ferries carry hikers and gear across the Gordon River, at the start of the south end, and across Nitinat Narrows, about halfway along the trail. Take some cash for fares.

The Canadian Parks Service sells a good West Coast Trail map. Tide tables for Tofino are needed to help with decisions about beach hiking.

South-end starters begin at Port Renfrew, about a hundred kilometres on Highway 14 from Victoria. Various attempts have been made in the past to provide public transportation between Victoria and Port Renfrew: check Travel Infocentres or the Canadian Parks Service. Hikers starting at the north end can catch the M.V. *Lady Rose* from Port Alberni to Bamfield and take a shuttle bus, or walk, five kilometres to the trail head at Pachena Bay. Gravel roads of about a hundred kilometres run to Pachena from Port Alberni and from Youbou, on Cowichan Lake.

Entire books have been written about the West Coast Trail. The recommended reading section at the back of this book will help you plan your hike. This journey is a serious undertaking and requires careful planning. Weather can be abysmal for the entire trip. Trail conditions are extremely

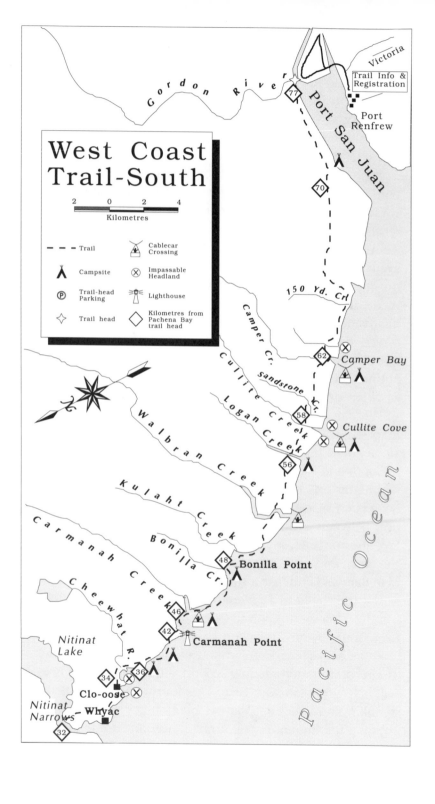

variable and no services are available. There are many minor hazards and some major ones, such as the possibility of getting stranded by high tide at the base of cliffs, or slipping into a surge channel.

An alternative to hiking the entire trail is to do only the northern section between Pachena and Nitinat Narrows. Considered by many to be the more scenic half, it definitely is less arduous than the southern end. An enjoyable four-to-five-day hike lets hikers experience much of the trail and still allows time for exploration of beaches near the campsites.

From the north end the first twelve kilometres of trail are wide, practically a road (part of it was a lighthouse supply road in years past). It passes Pachena Point Lighthouse at kilometre ten and Sea Lion Rocks, where sea lions haul out year round. A short side trail leads to a viewpoint overlooking these rocks, which may have several hundred sea lions hauled out at a time. The forested route is not strenuous but is up and down.

Michigan Creek, at kilometre twelve, has good campsites and a sand and gravel beach with tide pools. From here the beach can be followed two kilometres to the Darling River at kilometre fourteen where a cablecar carries hikers across the stream. There are good campsites here and many hikers use this as their first stop on the trip south.

Much of the beach can be hiked between the Darling and Klanawa rivers, an extremely scenic part of the trip, with tide pools, waterfalls, sandstone shelves, crashing surf; all the stuff one expects the West Coast Trail to be.

There is another cable crossing over the Klanawa at kilometre twenty-three. From here south to the journey's highlight, Tsusiat Falls at kilometre twenty-five, the trail moves into forest. The Tsusiat River plunges eighteen metres directly to a pool on the beach. It is, naturally, a very popular place to camp. Many people wash in the pool: use biodegradable soap. It's best, in fact, to resist the temptation of washing under the waterfall. Take a pot of water and bathe at least thirty metres from the falls.

If tides are low enough you can hike the beach from Tsusiat almost to Nitinat Narrows, at kilometre 32.5. You must return to the trail at Tsuquadra and Tsusiat points, and possibly other places, depending on tides.

Nitinat Narrows forms a natural boundary separating the northern section of the trail from the southern. Except for a short time at slack tide, the water roars through, creating extremely dangerous currents. Local Indians ferry hikers across Nitinat Narrows for a fee.

You can alternate between beach and forest for much of the 13.5 kilometres from Nitinat Narrows to Carmanah Creek. A cable car crosses the mouth of the creek. Upstream Canada's largest known Sitka spruce trees are protected within the 3,592-hectare Carmanah Pacific Provincial Park.

With a low tide the sandy beaches may be used for the seven-kilometre walk between Carmanah and Walbran creeks. At kilometre fifty-three Walbran Creek drains the Walbran Valley, an environmental hotspot of the nineties as logging threatens its old growth.

From Walbran to Logan Creek, at kilometre fifty-six, you can walk the beach but Adrenaline Surge, just north of Logan Creek, has claimed the life of at least one camper who attempted to cross it at high tide. Rocks here, even at low tide, may be slippery: you can take the forest route and cross Logan Creek on a suspension bridge.

The beach beyond Logan Creek can be tough slogging and many hikers prefer the trail to Camper Bay, at kilometre sixty-two. Some seasoned West Coast Trail hikers say Camper Bay, with spectacular ocean and mountain views, rivals Walbran as the most scenic campsite on the trail. From Camper bay to the south end of the trail you can walk the beach for short stretches at low tides: watch for incoming tides.

At kilometre seventy-seven the operator of a ferry across the Gordon River, at Port Renfrew, will gladly take more of your cash.

DELLA FALLS

• **Feature:** Highest waterfalls in Canada • **Usual Access:** Boat and backpack • **Time Required:** Minimum two days • **Nearest Highway:** Highway 4 • **Best Time To Visit:** May through October • **Maps:** NTS 1:50,000 92F/05

DELLA FALLS, at 440 metres the highest waterfalls in Canada, are in the remote southern section of Strathcona Provincial Park, near the city of Port Alberni. They can be reached by travelling twenty-eight kilometres up Great Central Lake, then hiking another sixteen kilometres to the base of the falls.

People who paddle to the trail head should beware of sudden gusts on Great Central, a narrow, steep-sided lake where winds funnel up from the head of Alberni Inlet. This lake is a reservoir and water levels are often artificially raised, covering beaches and other safe take-out spots. The trail follows Drinkwater Creek, which is fed by dozens of streams and waterfalls as it descends from Della Falls. This trip could be done overnight from Port Alberni, but squally weather on the lake could add two or three days — be prepared to wait out weather.

The lake is reached from Port Alberni by taking Highway 4 to the Sproat Lake Provincial Park turnoff, ten kilometres west of town, and following signs to Great Central. Rental boats may be available or arrangements for transportation to and from the trail head may be made at a local resort on the lake.

Near the end of the trail are the first views of the falls, but unfortunately, the entire cascade is not visible. To see most of the waterfall, and the tarn in the cirque above, hike up the Love Lake Trail, which ascends the opposite side of the valley from the falls. This trail leaves the Della Falls Trail just five hundred metres before the falls. It adds another two to three hours to the trip and is a steep route. For the best

One of three cascades in Della Falls.

view of the falls, charter a plane from Port Alberni.

LONG BEACH

• **Feature:** Long unspoiled beaches • **Usual Access:** Roadside access • **Time Required:** Two to seven days • **Nearest Highway:** Highway 4 • **Best Time To Visit:** Year round

LONG BEACH is just one in a series of beaches within Pacific Rim National Park, on the southwest coast of Vancouver Island. This is the island's primary natural attraction, with broad sandy shores, rocky headlands, pounding surf, tide pools, and forests of ferns, ancient cedars, hemlock, and Sitka spruce. More than half a million visitors come each year to watch the surf and sunsets. They come for summer sun; they come for winter storms.

From Parksville, take Highway 4, 138 kilometres to the Ucluelet-Tofino Junction. Going north (right) from the junction will take you to Pacific Rim National Park. Long Beach is seventeen kilometres from the junction.

Beachcombing is the most popular activity here. The ocean surf constantly washes up treasures to be examined, then left for the next explorers, or for the sea and sand to reclaim. The park's interpretation centre at Wickaninnish Bay offers a glimpse of the natural, historic, and native features of southwest Vancouver Island. Audio-visual presentations, talks, and slide shows are given here, and the centre is often a starting point for naturalist tours to various parts of the park. There's excellent beach walking below the interpretive centre, and trails to Florencia Bay and Combers Beach begin here.

Near the north end of the park the viewpoint at Radar Hill, accessible by wheelchair, offers a panoramic view of the coastline and forested mountains. It's a great place to watch a sunset, or migrating whales. Bring warm clothes.

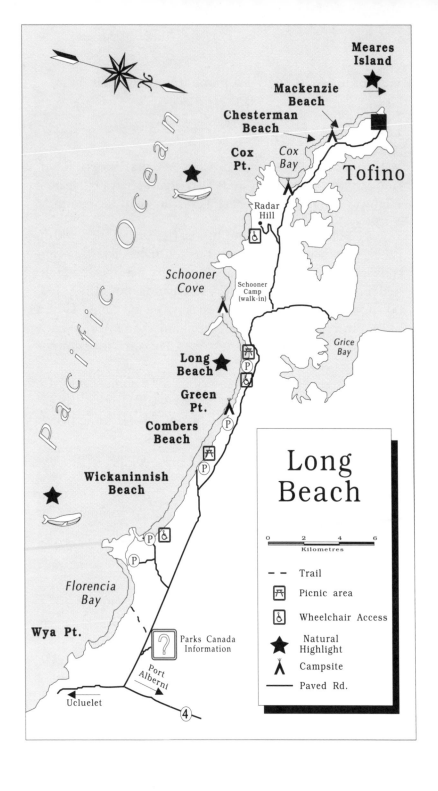

Meares
Island

Mackenzie
Beach

Chesterman
Beach

Cox
Pt.

Cox
Bay

Tofino

Radar
Hill

Pacific Ocean

Schooner
Cove

Schooner
Camp
(walk-in)

Grice
Bay

Long
Beach

Green
Pt.

Combers
Beach

Wickaninnish
Beach

Florencia
Bay

Wya Pt.

Parks Canada
Information

Port
Alberni

Ucluelet

4

Long
Beach

0   2   4   6
Kilometres

- - -   Trail

🏕   Picnic area

♿   Wheelchair Access

★   Natural
Highlight

⋀   Campsite

———   Paved Rd.

The Shorepine Bog Trail, also wheelchair accessible, is an eight-hundred-metre-long boardwalk through a poorly-drained area, home to many fascinating species of plants, including the carnivorous sundew (not to worry, it's tiny and eats only bugs). Details on other trails are available at park headquarters or the Interpretation Centre.

Camping in the park is limited. There are usually long summer line-ups at a drive-in campground at Green Point. A hike-in campsite, at Schooner Cove, is accessible via a one-kilometre long trail. Private campgrounds outside the park boundaries are available. Travel Infocentres throughout B.C. can provide details on campgrounds and other accommodations near the villages of Tofino and Ucluelet, at opposite ends of Long Beach.

An area of diverse habitats, Long Beach supports a variety of wildlife. Whales are often seen, especially during the spring migration of the Pacific gray whales. Sea lions, seals, and many species of seabirds are seen offshore and charter boats out of Tofino and Ucluelet provide a closer look.

On the beach itself are speedy little sandpipers, gulls, and terns, which often forage under the watchful eyes of bald eagles. Rocky areas are good places to see the black oyster-catcher, a crow-sized shorebird with a long red bill, or the beautiful blue and white harlequin ducks. Over 240 species of birds have been sighted in the park, situated on the Pacific flyway.

Small mammals such as raccoons, otters, and mink share the woods and beaches with black bears and blacktail deer. Wolves and cougars, also park residents, are rarely seen.

GRAY WHALE MIGRATION

• **Feature:** Pacific gray whales • **Usual Access:** Boat charters and shore • **Time Required:** Half to full day from Tofino-Ucluelet • **Nearest Highway:** Highway 4 • **Best Time To**

Visit: March to May • **Charts:** 3640 Clayoquot Sound, Lennard Island to Estevan Point 1:77,500; 3648 Clayoquot Sound (Northwest Portion) 1:36,500; 3649 Clayoquot Sound (Southeast Portion) 1:40,000

EVERY SPRING about twenty-one thousand Pacific gray whales return to Alaska from wintering grounds in Mexico's Baja California. They hug the shore along the west coast of Vancouver Island, stopping to rest and feed in the shallow waters near Ucluelet and Tofino. Whale watchers also make the annual migration to this area, either kayaking or taking commercial tours from Tofino or Ucluelet for close looks at these great creatures.

Canadian whale-watching guidelines suggest boaters stay at least one hundred metres from whales, but the whales don't know the rules and often surface alongside boats. Occasionally "friendlies" will rub the side of a boat and allow people to pat them, but these encounters are rare at Long Beach.

Whales are the largest marine species in the area, but you can see a fascinating array of other wildlife during a whale tour. Sea lions haul out on rocks off the coast. Seabird colonies, with thousands of nesting birds such as auklets and tufted puffins are in the area in summer. Tour boats often pass by these sites.

MEARES ISLAND

• **Feature:** Old-growth forest • **Usual Access:** Boat • **Time Required:** Day trip • **Nearest Highway:** Highway 4 • **Best Time To Visit:** Year round • **Charts:** 3640 Clayoquot Sound, Lennard Island to Estevan Point 1:77,500; 3649 Clayoquot Sound (Southeast Portion) 1:40,000

MEARES ISLAND, a total of eighty-six square kilometres, lies in Clayoquot Sound, dominating the tiny Vancouver

Island village of Tofino. An environmental hot spot, natives and locals are fighting to rescue the island's magnificent forests — including Canada's largest western red cedar — from the woodman's axe. People of all ages can board a boat in Tofino, hike a rain forest trail on Meares, and be picked up an hour or two later. Signs around Tofino indicate where to book a trip.

Wear gumboots or waterproof hiking shoes and carry water and wet-weather gear: this is, after all, a rain forest. The lushness of the forest, and the realization that people have depended on it for thousands of years, take on a deeper meaning when you experience it first-hand.

Kayakers often stop at Meares during trips to Hot Springs Cove and other Clayoquot Sound destinations. Rentals are available in Tofino.

HOT SPRINGS COVE

• **Feature:** Hot springs • **Usual Access:** Kayak, fly-in, or boat charters • **Time Required:** Full day from Tofino • **Nearest Highway:** Highway 4 • **Best Time To Visit:** Year round • **Charts:** 3640 Clayoquot Sound, Lennard Island to Estevan Point 1:77,500; 3648 Clayoquot Sound (Northwest Portion) 1:36,500; 3649 Clayoquot Sound (Southeast Portion) 1:40,000

LOCATED ON THE WEST coast of Vancouver Island, thirty-two kilometres north of Tofino, these springs are in Maquinna Provincial Park. They are the only known hot springs on Vancouver Island. Unlike other hot springs, they come with an ocean view, being right at the edge of the beach. There is no development of the six natural pools which run at about 50 degrees Celsius. There is even a waterfall for hot (soapless) showers. A two-kilometre trail from a government wharf runs through the bush to the springs.

Kayakers usually launch at the government wharf in Tofino. From here they generally take the scenic outside route, west of Vargas and Flores islands during fair weather. They save the sheltered eastern side for stormy conditions when swells on the outside get too big. Though the inside route is longer, novices would be wise to take it even in good weather. Rentals and guided kayak trips are available in Tofino.

Visitors shouldn't expect seclusion: it's a popular place, even in the winter. You might get lucky and have it all to yourself, especially during bad winter weather when the soothing waters are even more appreciated.

There is camping in the park and day trips may be arranged with charter boats or float plane companies in Tofino.

STRATHCONA MEADOWS

• **Feature:** Alpine ridge and mountain scenery • **Usual Access:** Day hikes • **Time Required:** Two to twelve hours from trail head • **Nearest Highway:** Highway 4 • **Best Time To Visit:** August and September • **Maps:** NTS 1:50,000 92F/05

STRATHCONA PROVINCIAL PARK, B.C.'s oldest, created in 1911, is located at the centre of Vancouver Island. More than 210,000-hectares, its boundaries encompass a multitude of natural highlights from alpine meadows, the highest mountain on the island, and beautiful waterfalls including Canada's highest, rating an extended visit. Highlights in this huge park are in widely separated areas requiring varying levels of effort to reach. The park has a large deer population, as well as elk, wolves, cougars, and smaller animals.

Flower enthusiasts are drawn to the park for its wildflowers. Two popular destinations in the park are Marble Meadows, a backpacking trip, and Paradise Meadows, more suited for a family day hike. These meadows are located in the two main areas of the park with visitors' facilities; Buttle Lake and Forbidden Plateau respectively.

Hikers should carry water and extra clothing. Keep an eye on the weather: it is easy to lose your way in poor visibility. Many areas are exposed and landmarks are few when clouds obscure distant peaks.

Marble Meadows is located in the Buttle Lake area of the park, west of Buttle Lake. Of the park's many wildflower meadow areas, Marble Meadows is the best known.

From Campbell River take Highway 28 west for forty-eight kilometres to Buttle Lake. Follow the road down the east side of the lake twenty-three kilometres to Karst Creek boat ramp. Here a boat is required to reach the mouth of Phillips Creek on the west side of Buttle Lake, where the trail begins. Canoes can be launched at Auger Point rest area just before Karst Creek, and are available for rent at the nearby Strathcona Park Lodge.

The 6.6-kilometre trail ascends 1,250 metres to the meadows. Three campsites are available; at the mouth of Phillips Creek, about halfway along the trail, and about three kilometres west of the plaque marking the end of the trail.

Marble Meadows' landscape consists of high open ridges dotted with small lakes, and multi-hued carpets of alpine flowers. Globeflowers, western anemones, paintbrush, and pink, white, and yellow heathers, are just a few of the flower species that form a changing mosaic as the season progresses.

Paradise Meadows Trail is the most popular access to the central Forbidden Plateau area of the park. Richly-flowered meadows, views of glaciers, mountains, forests, and lakes await the hiker.

From Courtenay follow the signs for Mount Washington Ski Area west on a gravel road. At kilometre-ten turn right onto the main logging road and travel twenty-five kilometres to the Forbidden Plateau ski area. Here the left branch of the road continues another kilometre to the Paradise

Meadows trail head. The right branch leads to private ski chalets. Park vehicles well clear of the travelled surface of the road.

The trail is an easy day hike of one-kilometre, climbing only 122-metres, suitable for varying levels of fitness and ages.

From Paradise Meadows a network of interconnecting trails leads through open meadows interspersed with stands of alpine fir, and past several tiny flower-rimmed lakes.

JOHNSTONE STRAIT ORCAS

• **Feature:** Wild killer whales • **Usual Access:** Boat charters, canoe, or kayak • **Time Required:** One to seven days • **Nearest Highway:** Highway 19 • **Best Time To Visit:** June through October • **Charts:** 3659 Broughton Strait 1:37,600; 3568 Johnstone Strait (Western Portion) 1:36,500

JOHNSTONE STRAIT, off northeast Vancouver Island, is the world's most reliable killer-whale-watching territory. Each year these intriguing leviathans patrol the strait and surrounding waters from about mid-June to early October, searching for salmon headed for spawning streams. Other whales, sea lions, seals, dolphins, and a multitude of birds share the strait with the killer whales.

Commercial whale-watching tours, some of which listen to whales through underwater microphones, are available in the boardwalk village of Telegraph Cove and from coastal communities nearby. Book ahead. Owners of power boats, canoes, kayaks, and operators of kayak tours usually launch at Telegraph Cove, about a seven-hour drive from the city of Victoria. There's a campsite at Telegraph Cove and accommodation at the north-island towns of Port Hardy and Port McNeill. Check Tourism B.C.'s *Accommodations* guide.

Perhaps the busiest whale-watching area is between

Telegraph Cove and Robson Bight. Whales are often seen as they enter the bight, which is a protected ecological reserve. They come here to rub on the gravel sea floor. Another attraction for them is salmon. The Tsitika River, running into Robson Bight, is an important salmon-producing stream, and is heating up as an environmental hotspot. It is being logged in its upper reaches and environmentalists contend that siltation will affect the salmon, as well as the rubbing beaches, ending the appeal for the whales. Boaters are not allowed to enter the bight when whales are present. Camping is not allowed.

CAPE SCOTT BEACHES

• **Feature:** Wilderness beaches • **Usual Access:** Day hikes-backpack • **Time Required:** One to seven days from Port Hardy • **Nearest Highway:** Highway 19 • **Best Time To Visit:** May to October • **Maps:** NTS 1:50,000 102I/09 • **Charts:** 3624 Cape Cook to Cape Scott 1:90,000

CAPE SCOTT is the extreme northwest tip of Vancouver Island. The shores around the cape have nine separate sandy beaches totalling twenty-three kilometres in length. Varying in length from a few hundred metres to 2.4 kilometres, they invite many days of exploration, marine life observation, and the relaxation that comes easily on an uncrowded seashore. Rocky headlands, some with fascinating tide pools, separate the stretches of sandy beach. Sixty-four kilometres of coastline encompassing all nine beaches, and both east and west sides of the cape, are part of the 15,054-hectare Cape Scott Provincial Park. San Josef Bay is an hour's hike from the parking lot but the other beaches are at least an overnight backpacking trip.

To reach the trail-head parking areas from Port Hardy, at the north end of Vancouver Island on Highway 19, follow

Cape Scott beaches on northern Vancouver Island.

signs along logging roads for sixty kilometres east. Travel this route with extreme caution as there is active logging on weekdays with trucks suddenly barrelling around corners.

San Josef Bay, a 2.5-kilometre walk, is the only reasonable day trip from Port Hardy. Here huge ferns and beautiful yellow arum (skunk cabbage) line a walkway to a sandy beach. The far end of the beach from the trail has an oriental aura when the mist rolls in, the rocky headland having stunted trees, gnarled and twisted, resembling bonsais. This is a good day hike for families as the trail is quite easy going. A paddle down the San Josef River to the beach is also a pleasant day or overnight trip. Campers can use the San Josef Bay Campground adjacent to the San Josef River.

Although San Josef Bay is not usually crowded, those wishing more solitude must pay the price of taking the main hiking trail to Cape Scott. This trail is legendary, frequently damp, and at times of heavy rain, a major mudsloggy mess.

The reward comes after a five-to-eight-hour backpack. Here you find the most popular camping areas on the beaches at Nels Bight, the longest beach in the park, Experiment Bight, and Nissen Bight. Camping is allowed at other beaches but these three have fresh water. Once boiled, the brownish water is safe to drink.

The hike in is 16.2 kilometres to Nissen Bight, 19.4 kilometres to Nels Bight, and 22.6 kilometres to Experiment Bight. For hikers not wishing to hike all the way in one day, there are campsites at Eric Lake, just 3.5 kilometres up the trail, or a kilometre beyond the Fisherman River, about eleven kilometres from the trail head. The trail in, despite boggy sections, is enjoyable. Forests of huge trees, bogs with fascinating flora, windswept areas with grotesquely shaped pines.

The beaches are separated by headlands with short con-necting trails so you can usually find an uncrowded one, even in mid-summer. Wildlife watchers see seabirds and seals, sea lions, deer, and black bears. Wildflowers special-ly adapted to endure salt air and sand are found at Guise Bay. Tide pools teem with life in the rocky areas, providing hours of enjoyment.

Although long periods of perfect weather are possible, this area can be swept by frequent storms accompanied by heavy wind and rain. Anchor tents solidly — a skinny little peg stuck loosely in the sand won't do. And have a good look around to ensure your camp is well above the high-tide line. Consulting a tide table before the trip is a good idea.

Icy snowmelt cools hikers on the trail to Black Tusk and Garibaldi Lake.

Southwestern B.C.

Southwest British Columbia, with its mountains, lakes and waterfalls, inlets, islands, and seashores, is one of the province's most accessible regions for outdoors people. From its major centre, Vancouver, many of the outdoor excursions can be done as day or weekend trips.

Highways radiate from the city, following the Fraser River and its infamous canyon, climbing beyond the fiordlike coast of Howe Sound into the Coast Mountains, or cutting through the Cascades toward interior B.C. Ferries connect the mainland with Vancouver Island and the Sunshine Coast, and Vancouver International Airport is the entry point for millions of travellers.

As particularly scenic areas like Garibaldi Park or Princess Louisa Inlet become increasingly popular, a growing number of out-back explorers are planning their trips for mid-week or the so-called off-seasons.

Highway 99, along the edge of Howe Sound, is probably the most interesting route for viewing natural highlights within a day's drive of Vancouver. Along the way is the second-largest granite rock face in the world, one of the highest waterfalls in Canada, extinct volcanoes, alpine meadows, and undeveloped hot springs. Highway 101, on the Sunshine Coast, accesses more remote marine areas, attracting kayakers and cruisers to Desolation Sound and Princess Louisa Inlet. The routes east through the Fraser Valley lead to large concentrations of bald eagles, the raging waters of

Southwestern British Columbia

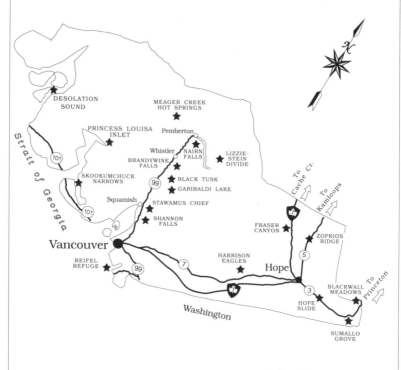

Strait of Georgia

DESOLATION SOUND

MEAGER CREEK HOT SPRINGS

PRINCESS LOUISA INLET

Pemberton

Whistler

NAIRN FALLS

LIZZIE-STEIN DIVIDE

BRANDYWINE FALLS

SKOOKUMCHUCK NARROWS

BLACK TUSK

GARIBALDI LAKE

Squamish

To Cache Cr.

To Kamloops

STAWAMUS CHIEF

SHANNON FALLS

FRASER CANYON

ZOPKIOS RIDGE

Vancouver

REIFEL REFUGE

HARRISON EAGLES

Hope

BLACKWALL MEADOWS

To Princeton

Washington

HOPE SLIDE

SUMALLO GROVE

Vancouver

—— Maintained highway

=== Forestry road

★ Natural highlight

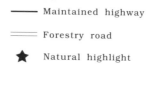

Kilometres

| 25 | 0 | 25 | 50 | 75 | 100 |

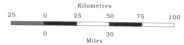

0   30

Miles

the Fraser Canyon, and easily accessible alpine meadows.

Two major provincial parks dominate this region. Garibaldi, largely a hiker's park, is an hour and a half north of Vancouver on Highway 99. Its mountain scenery is the best in the region. Manning, a good family park, is three hours west of Vancouver via Highway 3. There are lots of nature trails, canoeing, and accessible meadows.

The Fraser River delta is a major wildlife attraction. Thousands of snow geese and other migrating waterfowl stop here to rest or winter in extensive salt marshes south of Vancouver. Large mammals are not common in Southwestern B.C. but black bears and deer are seen in the more remote areas. There is a small population of grizzlies near Pemberton and in the Upper Stein Valley, and visitors to Manning Park may spot a moose or two.

Ease of access, large urban centres for accommodation and outfitting, good roads, an international airport, and proximity to the highlights and other tourist regions make this region a good place to begin exploring the province.

DESOLATION SOUND

- **Feature:** Warm sheltered waters and coastal scenery
- **Usual Access:** Kayak or other boat • **Time Required:** Three to ten days • **Nearest Highway:** Highway 101 • **Best Time To Visit:** May to October • **Charts:** 3594 Discovery Passage, Toba Inlet, and Connecting Channels 1:75,000

TWO CENTURIES AGO, the famous marine surveyor, Captain George Vancouver, did not find Desolation Sound impressive. He gave the area its misleading name, saying it was gloomy, lacking in marine life and wild edibles to sustain his crew. Modern-day visitors dispute his evaluation. The waterways and islands are among the most scenic on the southern B.C. coast, backdropped by the snow-capped peaks of the Coast Range rising well over two thousand metres above the sea. Contrary to Vancouver's assessment, there are oysters, prawns, crab, fish, and a variety of berries and edible plants. Deer and bear roam the thick coastal forests.

This is one of the most popular cruising and kayaking destinations on the B.C. coast. Desolation Sound Provincial Marine Park and Recreation Area, established in 1973, covers 8,256 hectares of islands and mainland. Its waters are among the warmest on the coast, often reaching 25.6 degrees Celsius. The sheltered waters between islands, and short crossings are ideal for kayakers, and during summer it is frequently calm. Crowded, at times, with power boaters and sailors, the sound is big enough for kayakers to get away from the cruisers and sailors, especially since those folks tend to gather at established anchorages.

B.C. Parks has moored garbage scows at the most scenic areas to help ensure boaters keep these waters clean. The most popular havens are Roscoe Bay, Prideaux Haven, Tenedos Bay, Portage Cove, Isabel Bay, and Grace Harbour. Some anchorages have walk-in campsites. With a little patience and careful reconnoitering, secluded camping areas may be found but there are few beaches here. The shoreline is mainly rocky with dense bush. A few small, grassy islets make excellent camps. Carry your own fresh water.

The usual take-off points for trips to Desolation Sound by small boaters are, Lund, and Okeover Arm, north of Powell River, and Cortes Island.

From Powell River, reached by car and passenger ferries from Vancouver or Courtenay, travel north twenty-three kilometres on Highway 101 to the tiny town of Lund. Supplies here are limited and pricey: buy them beforehand. From Lund it's a short trip through the scenic Copeland Islands and around the Malaspina Peninsula to Desolation Sound.

A more sheltered and direct route to Desolation Sound,

accessing anchorages at Isabel Bay and Grace Harbour, is from Okeover Arm. Follow Highway 101 north from Powell River seventeen kilometres, turn east and go four kilometres to the public wharf at Okeover Arm. Make sure that valuables are not left in vehicles parked here: vandalism has been a problem in recent years.

B.C. Ferries run to Powell River from Little River, near Courtenay on Vancouver Island. Mainland ferries from Horseshoe Bay connect to Sechelt Peninsula, then another ferry runs to the Powell River area. Cortes Island is reached by taking a ferry from Campbell River, on Vancouver Island, to Quadra Island, then driving across Quadra to a ferry running to Cortes. Kayakers usually launch at Squirrel Cove or Cortes Bay.

PRINCESS LOUISA INLET

• **Feature:** Scenic fiord • **Usual Access:** Boat or fly-in, charters available • **Time Required:** One to seven days • **Nearest Highway:** Highway 101 • **Best Time To Visit:** April through October • **Charts:** 3589 Jervis Inlet and Approaches 1:76,400

PRINCESS LOUISA INLET, projecting like a tiny appendix from the farthest reaches of Jervis Inlet, is considered by many as the B.C. coast's best inlet for inspiring a spiritual feeling. It is like a secret hideaway, the entrance barred by the turbulent rip tides of Malibu Rapids, and unlocked only briefly during slack tide. Once inside, the visitor is surrounded by one-thousand-metre-high granite walls, and a silence reminiscent of the great cathedrals of Europe. The entire length is only eight kilometres: its width only eight hundred metres.

The peaks of the Coast Range are snow-capped all year; consequently there are cascading threads of meltwater everywhere. The cliffs rise from the inlet floor, three hundred metres below the surface, to twenty-one hundred metres above sea level. There are usually at least sixty waterfalls cascading into the inlet: the most magical of times is after summer rains, when hundreds of fine white ribbons stream from the sheer precipices. The highlight for most visitors is Chatterbox Falls, a forty-metre cascade at the head of the inlet, site of Princess Louisa Provincial Marine Park. Once visited, it is usually revisited.

Before becoming a provincial park the falls and surrounding land were held under a trusteeship administered by the Princess Louisa International Society. This property was donated by James F. "Mac" MacDonald, who compared it to some of the world's most beautiful places, such as Yosemite and the fiords of Norway.

Aside from the scenery, visitors come for the warm water, often reaching 20 degrees Celsius, or higher, in summer. Indians knew about this and called it "Suivoolot," which means sunny and warm. Those who visit when it's sunny and warm, certainly experience one of the best natural highs the province has to offer.

To reach the inlet, most kayakers choose Irvines' Landing, near Pender Harbour on Sechelt Peninsula, as a launch site. It is advisable to plan a week for getting to the marine park, exploring the inlet, and returning to your launch site.

SKOOKUMCHUCK NARROWS

• **Feature:** Tidal rapids • **Usual Access:** Day hike • **Time Required:** Day trip from Sunshine Coast locations • **Nearest Highway:** Highway 101 • **Best Time To Visit:** Times of highest tide variations

SKOOKUMCHUCK NARROWS, near the entrance to Sechelt Inlet, constrict the huge volume of water gushing through at tide changes. This causes some of the most powerful currents on the coast, racing through at up to six-teen knots, forming three-metre standing waves. The sound of these rapids can be heard several kilometres away. Their force can suck a large power boat to the bottom and spit it back to the surface hundreds of metres downstream. Crazy kayakers who attempt to shoot these rapids are the bane of boaters who risk their lives attempting to rescue capsized paddlers.

Forget your kayak and take the hiking trail to the rapids. Take Highway 101, fifty kilometres north from Sechelt on the Sunshine Coast, then turn east to Egmont. Just before the village there is a turnoff to the right for Skookumchuck Narrows Provincial Park. From the parking lot a four-kilometre trail leads to viewpoints at the very edge of the turbulent waters. This is a pleasant approach to the rapids, hiking through cool dark forests with lush mosses and ferns, winter wrens and woodpeckers, and the occasional deer.

The tide changes from dead slack to a swift current in minutes, to major rapids in an hour. When the current is at its greatest, sit back on the flat rocks and enjoy, but keep children well away from the edge.

A small bay just before the viewing site offers incredible tidal-pool exploration at low tide. The creatures living here benefit from an enhanced nutrient flow due to the massive volumes of water passing through the narrows.

Camping is allowed here, but there are no developed campsites or services. Most people make this a day hike. There is camping nearby at Egmont.

SHANNON FALLS

• **Feature:** Waterfall • **Usual Access:** Roadside • **Time Required:** Half day from Vancouver • **Nearest Highway:** Highway 99 • **Best Time To Visit:** Year round • **Maps:** Outdoor Recreation Council — #14 Greater Vancouver-Squamish-

Shannon Falls, south of Squamish.

Lower Fraser Valley Region 1:100,000

THIS POPULAR PICNIC SPOT, an hour's drive north of Vancouver, features a series of three cascades which drop a total of 335 metres. In 1984 the provincial government bestowed park status on the small area around the falls. There is a very civilized walking trail to a viewing platform near the base of the cascades. Many people scramble up huge boulders for a closer view. Bear in mind, however that these boulders came from above. Also beware of slippery rocks near the base. There is a little-used hiking trail to the left of the falls, which leads to the top. It is a long steep journey, but the views are much better than from the established lookout at the base.

Take Highway 99 north from Vancouver's Horseshoe Bay, thirty-three kilometres to Britannia Beach, then continue seven kilometres to the Shannon Falls parking lot. Head towards the falls and you will find the walking trail.

STAWAMUS CHIEF

- **Feature:** Huge rock face • **Usual Access:** Roadside • **Time Required:** Half day from Vancouver • **Nearest Highway:** Highway 99 • **Best Time To Visit:** Year round • **Maps:** Outdoor Recreation Council - #14 Greater Vancouver-Squamish-Lower Fraser Valley Region 1:100,000

THIS IS THE SECOND-LARGEST granite monolith in the world, next to the Rock of Gibralter. Its huge west face, 560 metres high, is renowned the world over as a supreme invitation to rock climbers. Travellers along Highway 99 often stop at the pulloff near the base of the cliff to watch the flyspecks inching their way up the overhanging slabs. This is the defining natural feature of the town of Squamish, an hour north of Vancouver. Trails lead to the flat-topped summit for views over Howe Sound, and there are routes directly

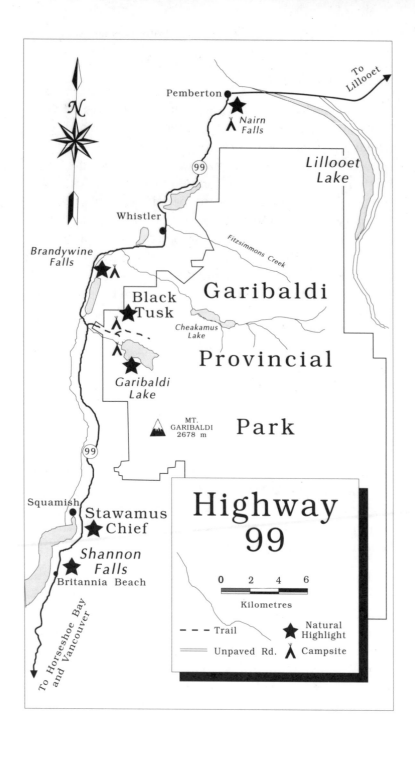

up the face.

Take Highway 99 north from West Vancouver's Horseshoe Bay for thirty-three kilometres to Britannia Beach; continue ten kilometres to a stop of interest pullout on the right.

A hiking trail leads to the top, with branches to the three main summits. The trail may be accessed from the viewpoint area, or from Shannon Falls Provincial Park, 1.2 kilometres south. From the viewpoint, find an old dirt road leading to a quarry just south of the Chief. The trail begins at the east end, going up some old stairs where it intersects the route from Shannon Falls. The trail continues up, with signs at major junctions indicating the routes to First, Second, and Third peaks.

The First Peak Trail branches left off the trail to Second Peak. First Peak Trail comes to a dead end, where a view over the edge is quite invigorating for some, terrifying for others. Exercise extreme caution here as balance can easily be lost near the edge. Take a step or two back before using a camera or binoculars. In damp weather the rocks are slippery. This is a dangerous place.

Hikers may wish to bypass First Peak, and continue on the right branch to Second Peak, which offers alternatives for the return trip to the parking lot. From Second Peak follow the ridge to North Gully, which separates Second and Third peaks. The trail branches near the top of the gully, the left fork continuing to Third Peak, the right returning to the main trail and the parking lot.

Distances are 6.4 kilometres to First Peak, 9.5 kilometres to Second Peak, and 11 kilometres to Third Peak. Elevation gain for any of the three peaks is over 600 metres.

THE BLACK TUSK

- **Feature:** Volcanic plug • **Nearest Highway:** Highway 99
- **Usual Access:** Backpack • **Time Required:** Overnight

The Black Tusk, not a place for hikers who fear heights.

from Vancouver • **Best Time To Visit:** Late July to September • **Maps:** NTS 1:50,000 92G/09; BC Parks brochure for Garibaldi Park; Outdoor Recreation Council - #3 Whistler/Garibaldi Region 1:100,000

THE BLACK TUSK, at 2,315 metres, is a summit north of Garibaldi Lake, topped with a bare rock fang protruding from surrounding gentle slopes. Thought to be the lava plug of an extinct volcano, it's the most distinctive feature of the landscape between Garibaldi Lake and the Whistler area. Below the stunning summit are extensive meadows with wildflowers in mid-summer that draw thousands of visitors each year. Part of the appeal is its proximity to Vancouver, less than two hours' drive away.

A good trail leads to the Black Tusk, making a long day trip from Vancouver. Campsites are available in the nearby meadows.

Views from the summit are tremendous. Mount Garibaldi, at 2,678 metres the highest in the park, shimmers in the south; the Tantalus Range highlights the west, Castle Towers with its glaciers commands the east, and the 2,135-metre Whistler Mountain in the north completes the 360 degree panorama. Most hikers can manage the final exposed scramble to the top of the tusk, making it one of the most popular hikes in the lower mainland.

To reach the trail head for the hike to the summit, take Highway 99 north from Vancouver sixty-four kilometres to the town of Squamish. Continue north thirty-seven kilometres to the signed turnoff for Black Tusk. A paved road leads 2.4 kilometres to the Rubble Creek parking lot where the trail begins.

The trail gains elevation steadily through a wonderful forest of huge old trees. Start early to avoid crowds and heat, especially during the peak wildflower season. After six kilometres there is a junction, with the left fork leading to Taylor Camp and Black Tusk, the other to Garibaldi Lake.

Either camp is suitable as a base for a trip to the Black Tusk. Taylor Camp is more accessible to alpine meadows, but some prefer the lakeshore scenery at Garibaldi Lake.

From Taylor Meadows follow the signs past the junction with the trail from Garibaldi Lake, and continue climbing until the grassy meadows give way to the dry volcanic ridge, with the tusk looming ahead. The trail is easy to follow and very well travelled. After crossing a talus slope below the summit block, there is a rather exposed step or two to the steep chimney leading to the top. This is where many will, or should, call it a day. It is no place for anyone afraid of heights, as it entails using hands and feet carefully, in a very exposed situation. There are plenty of holds but a slip here could be disastrous. It's wise to use a rope. The chimney is not long, and terminates at the lower end of the summit slope, where a trail leads to the top. The views are worth the effort.

It is even harder descending the chimney. Go down the way you come up. There are a couple of similar-looking gullies that end in dropoffs, so make sure of your location before committing yourself.

GARIBALDI LAKE

• **Feature:** Alpine scenery • **Nearest Highway:** Highway 99 • **Time Required:** Overnight from Vancouver • **Usual Access:** Backpack • **Best Time To Visit:** July to September • **Maps:** NTS 1:50,000 92G/09; BC Parks brochure - Garibaldi Park; Outdoor Recreation Council - #3 Whistler/Garibaldi Region 1:100,000

GARIBALDI LAKE and its environs entice scenery lovers from around the world. An incredible blue tint that changes with the seasons, the lake is the focal point of Garibaldi Provincial Park. Snowcapped summits rising to more than

2,500 metres surround the lake. Glaciers flow from the mountainsides, almost reaching the lakeshore, their silty meltwaters contributing to the startling colour of the lake. Signs of volcanic activity abound. The volcanic plug of the Black Tusk commands the area north of the lake, while the mesa-like flat-topped Table Mountain, and the gigantic white bulk of the park's highest peak, Mount Garibaldi at 2,678 metres, predominate in the south. There are cinder cones, basalt columns and lava dams. The finest wilderness alpine meadows within a half day of Vancouver are a half-hour hike above the lake. This is unquestionably one of the most beautiful natural areas in Canada, if not the world.

Thirty thousand years ago the eruption of Mount Price caused lava to come into contact with the remains of a glacial ice sheet. The lava cooled, forming a solid rock wall, now called the Barrier. This transformed the upper valley, creating an enclosed basin eventually filled to a depth of three hundred metres with meltwater from receding glaciers. Volcanic activity has stopped and the ice sheet has largely disappeared, but evidence of ancient times remain in the dramatic landscapes nearby. Mount Garibaldi, a volcano partly built on top of a glacier, dominates the landscape. Across the lake to the east the Sphinx and Sentinel glaciers, remnants of the last great ice sheet, fall from the flanks of Castle Towers and Sphinx Mountain.

Part of the area's appeal is due to its proximity to Vancouver. An hour's drive (sixty-four kilometres) north of Vancouver on Highway 99 is the town of Squamish. From Squamish, Highway 99 leads north thirty-seven kilometres to the signed turnoff for the Black Tusk area. A paved road goes east 2.4 kilometres to the Rubble Creek parking lot where the trail begins.

The trail gains elevation steadily through an old forest. Get an early start to avoid crowds and heat, especially during the peak wildflower season in mid-summer. After six kilometres there is a junction with the left fork going to Taylor

Meadows and Black Tusk, and the right to Garibaldi Lake. A few metres past the junction a path to the right leads to an excellent view of the Barrier. The main trail continues to climb until it reaches the top of the Barrier. It then skirts tiny Barrier Lake and emerald-hued Lesser Garibaldi Lake. Just past the eight-kilometre mark is another trail junction, the left fork heads to Taylor Meadows and the right to Garibaldi Lake. At 8.5 kilometres the trail crosses a bridge over Rubble Creek where there's a breathtaking view of the lake and the glaciated peaks on the far side.

The Battleship Islands Campground, final destination for most hikers, is just five hundred metres farther along the lakeshore. Most overnight campers stay at this campground, beside the lake at the end of the Garibaldi Lake Trail. This makes a good basecamp; from here there are day hikes of varying difficulty. The most popular are to Black Tusk, Panorama Ridge, and Taylor Meadows, known for spectacular wildflower displays in mid to late summer.

In order to maintain the area's appeal, it has been protected as part of the Black Tusk Nature Conservancy, within Garibaldi Provincial Park. Camping is allowed only at designated sites, open fires are prohibited, hunting or commercial activities are banned, and motorized vehicles are prohibited. Visitors to this area are asked to stay on trails, and never approach or feed animals in the area, especially bears.

BRANDYWINE FALLS

• **Feature:** Waterfall • **Usual Access:** Roadside - short walk • **Time Required:** Optional • **Nearest Highway:** Highway 99 • **Best Time To Visit:** Year round • **Maps:** Outdoor Recreation Council - #3 Whistler/Garibaldi Region 1:100,000

BRANDYWINE FALLS are a seventy-metre-high waterfall on Brandywine Creek, a kilometre above Daisy Lake. It is one of the most popular natural highlights of the Whistler area, a one-and-a-half-hour drive north of Vancouver. Trails lead to viewpoints overlooking the falls, the centrepiece of Brandywine Falls Provincial Park.

Apparently the stakes in a bet over the height of the falls, brandy and wine, resulted in its name.

A visit to the falls is a good picnic outing from Vancouver or Whistler. There is also camping for a nightly fee in the park. Hiking trails lead to Brandywine Meadows and Brandywine Mountain, providing more challenging activities during an overnight visit to the falls. Nearby Daisy Lake has good swimming.

Take Highway 99 north from Vancouver sixty-four kilometres to the town of Squamish, continue north, thirty-seven kilometres to the park.

NAIRN FALLS

• **Feature:** Waterfall • **Usual Access:** Roadside • **Time Required:** Full day from Vancouver • **Nearest Highway:** Highway 99 • **Best Time To Visit:** Year round

SOUTH OF PEMBERTON the Green River plunges sixty metres in Nairn Falls Provincial Park. The falls makes a good day trip from Vancouver. Campers may use the park campground, which has eighty-eight sites.

From Horseshoe Bay take Highway 99 north forty-four kilometres to Squamish at the head of Howe Sound, continue north, eighty-four kilometres to Nairn Falls Provincial Park.

LIZZIE-STEIN DIVIDE

• **Feature:** Alpine lakes and meadows • **Usual Access:** Backpack, long day hike • **Time Required:** Two days

• **Nearest Highway:** Highway 99 • **Best Time To Visit:** Late July to early October • **Maps:** NTS 92J/01; B.C. Forest Service Recreation Sites - Lillooet and area

THIS EXTENSIVE ALPINE area has been popular for years with residents of the Vancouver area, and now the access has been made almost too easy. It is located above the eastern shore of Lillooet Lake, south of Pemberton. Roads lead in to Lizzie Lake, from where the wilderness terrain rising to the divide above the lake can be explored on day hikes or overnight trips. There are numerous small lakes and tarns, highlighted by Tundra Lake, one of the most beautiful in B.C. Wildflowers abound here, and there are enough day hikes to fill up a ten-day trip without descending into the valleys below.

The tantalizingly named Gates of Shangri-La is a narrow defile between Lizzie Lake and the divide, featuring all three varieties of mountain heather, as well as many other wildflowers, marmots, and pikas (rock rabbits). A privately-owned cabin at the edge of the meadows is open to the public and should be left as you found it. It makes a good base of operations for exploring the alpine area. Other lakes in the area are Arrowhead, Iceberg, Sapphire, and London.

From Pemberton on Highway 99 take the road east to Mount Currie, go right on Duffey Lake Road, and at kilometre 10.5 turn south on the east-side road along Lillooet Lake, then continue south for thirty-three kilometres to Lizzie Creek. Take the next logging road on the left, keeping right at the forks until the campsite is reached at Lizzie Lake. From the east end of the lake take the trail to the alpine.

MEAGER CREEK HOT SPRINGS

• **Feature:** B.C.'s largest hot springs • **Usual Access:** Roadside • **Time Required:** Day trip from Vancouver • **Nearest**

Highway: Highway 99 • **Best Time To Visit:** Year round • **Maps:** B.C. Forest Service Recreation Sites - Lillooet and area

MEAGER CREEK HOT SPRINGS is a favourite spot for soakers from Whistler, Squamish, and as far away as Vancouver. The water, at 38 degrees Celsius, is especially soothing for cross-country skiers who make the springs a day trip destination in winter. They are located about forty kilometres north of Pemberton near the confluence of Meager Creek and the Lillooet River.

From Horseshoe Bay take Highway 99 north to Whistler then continue north thirty-five kilometres to Pemberton. To get to the springs during snow-free months take the Lillooet River Road to the confluence of Meager Creek and Lillooet River.

REIFEL REFUGE

• **Feature:** Waterfowl • **Usual Access:** Easy walks • **Time Required:** Half day from Vancouver • **Nearest Highway:** Highway 99 • **Best Time To Visit:** Fall-spring migrations • **Maps:** Outdoor Recreation Council - #14 Greater Vancouver-Squamish-Lower Fraser Valley Region 1:100,000

AS MANY AS FORTY THOUSAND snow geese pause in the Fraser River delta during late October and early November, on their annual migration south from Siberia to warmer climes. The best place to view this spectacle is at the George C. Reifel Migratory Bird Sanctuary, named after the man who once owned the property on Westham Island. A few minutes' drive from downtown Ladner there are pleasant walking trails along dikes and waterways which provide good opportunities for viewing more than 230 bird species. An admission fee is charged.

From Vancouver take Highway 99 south to Ladner. From

Ladner there are good signs to the sanctuary.

HARRISON RIVER EAGLES

• **Feature:** Large gathering of bald eagles • **Usual Access:** Roadside • **Time Required:** Optional • **Nearest Highway:** Highway 7 • **Best Time To Visit:** November to December • **Maps:** Outdoor Recreation Council - #11 Chilliwack-Hope-Skagit Region 1:100,000

EVERY WINTER hundreds of bald eagles congregate along the Chehalis and Harrison rivers to feast on the carcasses of dead salmon after the autumn spawn. Although poaching has made the eagles wary, there are excellent observation opportunities from the Harrison River bridge on Highway 7. More than four hundred eagles are known to frequent the area from November through December. Located in the Fraser Valley, just an hour and a half from

Bald eagles at salmon spawn on Harrison River.

Vancouver, it presents an opportunity to see a spectacular natural event on a leisurely day trip.

Take Highway 7 from Mission thirty-three kilometres to the Harrison River bridge. There are usually limited places to park on either side of the river near the bridge. There may be better viewing from the road to the Weaver Creek Fish Hatchery (turnoff five hundred metres west of the bridge).

There is private property and Indian land throughout the area: ask permission to walk on it.

FRASER CANYON

• **Feature:** River canyon • **Usual Access:** Roadside • **Time Required:** Half day • **Nearest Highway:** Highway 1 (Trans-Canada) • **Best Time To Visit:** Year round

THE FRASER CANYON is an infamous gorge on a stretch of the mighty Fraser River between Boston Bar and Yale. The huge water volume becomes confined between steep rock walls, unleashing its energy as whirlpools and rapids in a display of frightening power. The Trans-Canada Highway parallels the river through this section, where there are many viewpoints above raging waters. The best spot is Hell's Gate, where the water gushes through a thirty-four-metre defile with awesome fury. For a fee an aerial tramway takes visitors from the highway down to the river, crossing over the rapids.

Even more thrilling is a white-water rafting trip from Boston Bar to Yale with one of several tour operators. Scuzzy Rock, China Bar, and Hell's Gate rapids are skillfully negotiated by river guides using motorized inflatable rafts. There is no better way to gain respect for the river's power than on one of these one-day adventures.

Fraser Canyon.

HOPE SLIDE

• **Feature:** Landslide • **Usual Access:** Roadside • **Time Required:** One half hour from Hope • **Nearest Highway:** Highway 3 • **Best Time To Visit:** Year round • **Maps:** Outdoor Recreation Council - #8 Princeton-Manning-Cathedral Region 1:100,000

EARLY ON JANUARY 9, 1965, forty-six million cubic metres of mountainside came thundering down, at 160 kilometres an hour, into the valley of Nicolum Creek, outside the city of Hope. There was a highway through the valley, and four people were killed. Two of the bodies still lie under the rubble, over which the new Hope-Princeton Highway is built. There is a viewpoint beneath the scar of bare rock lying exposed. Although not a beautiful sight or an event to celebrate, it does illustrate the dramatic force of nature.

From Hope take Highway 3, eighteen kilometres east to the Hope Slide viewpoint.

SUMALLO GROVE

• **Feature:** Giant cedars • **Usual Access:** Roadside • **Time Required:** Half day from Hope • **Nearest Highway:** Highway 3 • **Best Time To Visit:** Year round • **Maps:** Outdoor Recreation Council - #11 Chilliwack-Hope-Skagit Region 1:100,000

THIS DAY-USE AREA, along the Sumallo River, in the southwestern portion of Manning Provincial Park, is a shaded grove of huge western red cedars. It's a peaceful fishing and picnic spot. The greenery alongside the winding river is home to many species of birds, including warblers, towhees, and thrushes. Winter wrens sing in the tall forest, also home to woodpeckers and owls.

From Hope travel on Highway 3, 25.8 kilometres to the

Sumallo Grove turnoff. The parking area is a couple of hundred metres through the forest.

The Skagit River Trail begins here and follows the river for 14.5 kilometres to the Silver Skagit Road. Most hikers backpack in for about an hour, establish a basecamp, then day hike to the trail end and back. Along the way there is an ecological reserve featuring large cedars and Douglas firs, and the endangered wild rhododendron which blooms in mid-June.

BLACKWALL PEAK MEADOWS

• **Feature:** Alpine meadows • **Usual Access:** Roadside • **Time Required:** Day trip from Vancouver • **Nearest Highway:** Highway 3 • **Best Time To Visit:** Late July to early August • **Maps:** NTS 1:50,000 92H/02; BC Parks brochure - Manning Park; Outdoor Recreation Council - #8 Princeton-Manning Cathedral Region 1:100,000

THESE SPECTACULAR SUBALPINE MEADOWS are the major mid-summer attraction of Manning Provincial Park, a three-hour drive from Vancouver. The gently rolling terrain stretches twenty-four kilometres, from Blackwall Peak west to Nicomen Lake. This is B.C.'s most extensive meadow area that can be reached by road. Millions of wildflowers bloom from mid-July to late August.

For casual walkers, well maintained, short loop trails lead from parking areas, while a more arduous three-day hike is possible for backpackers. Open terrain offers sweeping panoramas of the Pasayten Wilderness, the jagged North Cascades of Washington state just a few kilometres to the south, and the heavily-forested hills between Manning Park and the Okanagan to the east. A visit to Manning Park is incomplete without a visit to the alpine meadows.

The meadows are a short drive from Manning Park Lodge.

Manning Park's Blackwall Peak meadows.

The lodge is on Highway 3, the Crowsnest Highway, sixty-seven kilometres east of Hope. Across Highway 3 from the main turnoff to the lodge is the road to Cascade Lookout. Follow this road fifteen kilometres uphill to the parking lot at its end. Within metres of the parking lot are the various trail heads, picnic tables, and a naturalist's hut where park interpreters provide information about routes and the fauna and flora of the meadows. About halfway up the road is a lookout where the pavement ends and becomes good gravel. Trailers should be left behind near the lodge; the road to the lookout is curvy. Daily interpretive walks are conducted on shorter trails, a good introduction to flower identification. A schedule of these walks is usually posted at the Manning Park Lodge parking lot.

Backcountry hikers can spend three days or more hiking across the entire length of meadows to Nicomen Lake, and beyond to Highway 3. There are three campsites along the way; Buckhorn Campground, just before the climb into the Three Brothers area, Kicking Horse Campground between the Third Brother and Fourth Brother mountains, and Nicomen Lake Campground.

Views from the section of trail from Buckhorn Camp to Kicking Horse Camp are spectacular. To the south on clear days, you can see the 3,285-metre peak of Washington's Mount Baker, in the North Cascades. From Nicomen Lake the trail descends through forest into Grainger Creek Valley. Hikers may be surprised by the shrill cries of hoary marmots, also known as whistlers. In the burn area along the Heather Trail, keen observers may even see the rare hawk owl.

Alpine meadows of Idaho Peak.

Okanagan-Kootenay

*O*kanagan-Kootenay is a region of big lakes, arid grasslands, rugged mountains, and wetlands. In the south-central and southeast sections of B.C., it has long been one of the province's most popular holiday destinations. The Okanagan receives more than two thousand hours of sunshine a year: it is one of the driest regions of Canada, with the country's only desert, near Osoyoos. Its long, narrow, warm-water lakes, flanked by irrigated farms and orchards, are legendary, filling the valley bottoms between the Thompson Plateau on the west and the Monashees on the east.

On the eastern side of the Okanagan Valley, the Monashee Mountains are the gateway to the Kootenays. Beyond the Monashees the Arrow Lakes reservoir is a widening of the Columbia River. Separating Arrow Lakes from Kootenay Lake are the high-horn peaks of the Selkirk Mountains, with glaciers, granite spires, and rainbow-hued meadows.

Highway 3, the Crowsnest, hugs the U.S. border through the southern side of this region all the way to the Rockies. Highway 97, which runs through the Okanagan Valley, is joined near Peachland by the Coquihalla Connector from the west. Highway 6 crosses the Monashees and runs into the heart of Kootenay country.

There are three major parks in Okanagan-Kootenay, Cathedral, Valhalla, and Kokanee Glacier Provincial Park. These parks are most popular with wilderness travellers, located high in the mountains, far above the narrow,

Okanagan-Kootenay

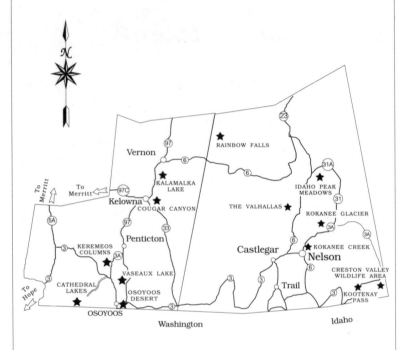

To Merritt

To Merritt

Vernon

RAINBOW FALLS

KALAMALKA LAKE

Kelowna

COUGAR CANYON

IDAHO PEAK MEADOWS

THE VALHALLAS

KOKANEE GLACIER

Penticton

KEREMEOS COLUMNS

Castlegar

KOKANEE CREEK

Nelson

VASEAUX LAKE

CRESTON VALLEY WILDLIFE AREA

CATHEDRAL LAKES

OSOYOOS DESERT

Trail

To Hope

OSOYOOS

KOOTENAY PASS

Washington

Idaho

Vancouver

——— Maintained highway

===== Forestry road

★ Natural highlight

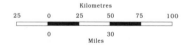

Kilometres

25   0   25   50   75   100

0   30
        Miles

populated valleys, where few undeveloped areas remain.

There is excellent wildlife viewing in this region. In parts of the Okanagan there are bighorn sheep, mountain goats, mule deer, and the unique species of the aridlands — such as Pacific rattlesnakes, spadefoot toads, lizards, and burrowing owls. The Okanagan, especially around Vaseux Lake, is one of the finest birding areas in Canada, with many species such as canyon wrens and painted buntings, found nowhere else in the country. Farther east, the Kootenays, with a moister climate, have significant waterfowl populations, especially in the Creston area. There are also large mammals such as black bears, the occasional grizzly, goats, elk, and deer.

The major hazard in this region is heat. The Okanagan is usually hot and sunny. Always carry plenty of water on day hikes, use sunscreen, and protect yourself with a sun hat. Read about heat injuries in a good first aid book and take precautions. While avoiding heat injuries, watch out for rattlesnakes. Chances are you won't ever see one, but just in case, be careful where you step, avoid sticking your limbs in holes in the ground, and never sit down without checking for snakes first. Always give way to warning rattles, never poke, prod or handle snakes, or any other wildlife for that matter.

This is a popular family holiday spot. On holidays and during summer celebrations small towns have been overtaken by hordes of young people. These are good times to get out of town and see the natural highs.

YELLOW PINE ECOLOGICAL RESERVE

• **Feature:** Yellow or ponderosa pine • **Usual Access:** Roadside • **Time Required:** Half day from Princeton • **Nearest Highway:** Highway 3 • **Best Time To Visit:** Year round

THE YELLOW, OR PONDEROSA PINE, has long been important to the B.C. lumber industry. Its long, yellow-green needles are gathered in groups of two or three that grow in tufts near the ends of branches. Its bright, reddish-orange bark is deeply furrowed, cracked and scaly.

A small grove of these lovely trees is preserved in a 32.4-hectare ecological reserve on Highway 3, three kilometres west of Princeton. Set aside as a representation of this area's flora, it's a pleasant place to stop for an hour or so when travelling the Hope-Princeton Highway. Watch for signs outside Princeton.

CATHEDRAL LAKES

• **Feature:** Alpine scenery • **Usual Access:** Backpack • **Time Required:** Three to five days • **Nearest Highway:** Highway 3 • **Best Time To Visit:** June to October • **Maps:** NTS 1:50,000 92H/01; Outdoor Recreation Council - #8 Princeton-Manning Cathedral Region 1:100,000; BC Parks brochure - Cathedral Lakes

THE 33,272-HECTARE Cathedral Provincial Park is located high in the Cascade Mountains between Manning Provincial Park and the Okanagan Valley. It's an alpine area with massive summits, valleys, and wide open spaces. Once you reach the main core area of Quiniscoe Lake a thirty-two-kilometre trail network accesses wilderness camping areas and picturesque views.

Wildlife, including bighorn sheep, black bears, mule deer, mountain goats, porcupines, and squirrels highlight the park. More than two hundred species of flowers display a patchwork of colour in the summer, along with the golden needles of alpine larch in autumn.

It is usually warm and sunny in summer. When moist air from the coast meets hot dry air from the interior,

Grimface Mountain on the Cathedral Rim Trail.

thunderstorms in late afternoon are common, enhancing the scenery with impressive displays of towering thunderheads.

There is a commercially-operated lodge at Quiniscoe Lake. Most backpackers use the provincial park campsites at Quiniscoe, and Pyramid lakes as bases for day hikes, to explore the highlights of the park including Cathedral Lakes and Stone City.

From Vancouver it is about a five-hour drive to Keremeos via the Trans-Canada Highway and Highway 3. From Keremeos travel south on the gravel Ashnola River Road to the Cathedral Lakes Resort parking lot, reserved for those who have booked a ride in the lodge vehicle to the core area of Quiniscoe Lake. Call Cathedral Lakes Resort and book a ride.

For those opting to hike into Quiniscoe Lake core area

there are several hiking routes. Trail heads can be reached via the Ashnola River Road.

The Lakeview Creek trail head is twenty-three kilometres up the Ashnola River Road, a few kilometres beyond the Cathedral Lakes Resort parking lot. Parking is available for about fifteen cars. Ensure vehicles are locked. Take your valuables. The sixteen-kilometre hiking trail up Lakeview Creek takes six to seven hours.

Another popular approach, requiring eight hours, is via Wall Creek Trail. The trail head is forty-eight kilometres up the Ashnola River Road.

A lesser used and longer approach is via the Ewart Creek Trail. Take the Ashnola River Road fourteen kilometres, turn left and follow this narrow, often rough road three kilometres to the parking lot at the trail head. The hike takes ten to twelve hours, and most people break up the trip by camping overnight at the Twin Buttes wilderness campsite.

Cathedral Lakes, consisting of Quiniscoe, Pyramid, Glacier, Lake of the Woods, and Ladyslipper, are connected by trails, providing easy day hikes through alpine meadows and spectacular rock formations. Pyramid, Glacier, and Lake of the Woods each may be reached from Quiniscoe in less than an hour and a half return. Ladyslipper Lake is a three-hour return trip with an elevation gain of 150 metres. Each lake has its own appeal, varying in colour, and set in a different aspect of the dramatic landscape.

Stone City is a fascinating open ridge, featuring house-sized, scattered granite outcroppings. Between these monoliths are patches of fragile alpine flowers, and grasses, specially adapted to the harshness of the alpine environment. Mountain goats frequent the area and generally cooperate with photographers.

Above the five beautiful lakes are spectacular views of the park, its many features to the north, and the Pasayten Wilderness of Washington state to the south. The plants, animals, and views are worth the easy day hike.

An interesting circuit trip, taking in Glacier Lake, Stone City, views of the Pasayten Wilderness, Ladyslipper Lake, and Pyramid Lake, provides an excellent all-day outing. From the south end of Quiniscoe Lake hike the trail to Glacier Lake then ascend the steep trail to the plateau above. The trail is well marked, the tread becoming fainter in the rocks above Glacier Lake, but cairns conspicuously indicate the route.

At the top of the climb, after five kilometres and 250 metres elevation gain, it intersects the Cathedral Rim Trail. Go left across the plateau, keeping a lookout for the herd of California bighorns in this area. Continue across the plateau past the basalt columns of the Devil's Woodpile to the massive grey boulders of Stone City.

The goats in this area seem to enjoy playing a form of hide and seek over the giant rocks, easily outmaneuvering hikers, in the rough terrain. From the eastern limits of Stone City descend the trail to Ladyslipper Lake into the larch forest, golden in fall, on through the spruce and pine around Pyramid Lake, and back to the starting point at Quiniscoe Lake.

The entire loop may be comfortably done in five hours or less but the fine views around Stone City beg for an extended lunch break, relaxing with the goats and scenery. Start early.

KEREMEOS COLUMNS

• **Feature:** Basalt columns • **Usual Access:** Day hike • **Time Required:** Full day from Keremeos • **Nearest Highway:** Highway 3A • **Best Time To Visit:** Year round • **Maps:** NTS 1:50,000 82E/0; Outdoor Recreation Council - #13 South Okanagan Region 1:100,000

KEREMEOS COLUMNS are an example of columnar

basalt, vertical hexagonal columns of rock fused together, resembling a bundle of six-sided sticks. They were formed when molten rock cooled slowly, during an era of volcanic activity more than thirty million years ago. The one-hundred-metre-wide outcropping of thirty-metre-high columns, is north of Keremeos, less than an hour's drive west from the Okanagan Valley. Oddly enough the columns are outside the boundaries of Keremeos Columns Provincial Park, but are visible from the park. On a five-kilometre hike to the columns you may encounter arid-country wildflowers such as bitterroot and buckwheat, found only in drier areas of the province.

From Keremeos take Highway 3A, north four kilometres to a cemetery, turn right and go east four hundred metres to a locked gate. The hike is six hours return, a hot trip in mid-summer: carry drinking water.

OSOYOOS POCKET DESERT

• **Feature:** Canada's only desert • **Usual Access:** Roadside
• **Time Required:** Half day from Osoyoos • **Nearest High-way:** Highway 97 • **Best Time To Visit:** Year round • **Maps:** Outdoor Recreation council - #13 South Okanagan Region 1:100,000

THE OSOYOOS AREA has the only true desert in Canada. Located at the most southern end of the Okanagan Valley, it's an extension of the Great Basin Desert of the United States, its northern section just making it over the border into Canada. This extremely dry and fragile area is fascinating for its many plants and animals, found nowhere else in the country.

From Osoyoos take Highway 97, north 7.5 kilometres to Road 22. Turn east for 1.5 kilometres, and park at an abandoned farm.

Significant nationally, this special feature has been set aside as a one hundred-hectare Ecological Reserve to preserve the flora and fauna and to maintain the natural state for scientific research. Overnight camping or any other disturbing activity is not allowed.

From the reserve there are excellent views of Osoyoos Lake and the surrounding desert terrain. Although appearing rather barren, it has rich plant and animal communities specially adapted to survive the harsh conditions.

A program is underway here to re-establish one of B.C.'s endangered species, the burrowing owl, a tiny raptor that nests in abandoned gopher or badger holes. Other species such as Pacific rattlesnakes, prickly pear cactus, rabbitbrush, and bitterroot may also be found.

VASEUX LAKE

• **Feature:** Bighorn sheep and birds • **Usual Access:** Roadside • **Time Required:** Day trip from Penticton or Osoyoos • **Nearest Highway:** Highway 97 • **Best Time To Visit:** April to November • **Maps:** Outdoor Recreation Council - #13 South Okanagan Region 1:100,000

THIS LAKE is named after the French word "vaseux" meaning muddy, or slimy, referring to silt deposits in the lake. Some say it's one of the finest birding areas in Canada. It's a small oasis in the desertlike terrain, lying between Okanagan Falls and Oliver in the south Okanagan Valley. There are trails and bird blinds for observing geese, swans, and ducks found in the marshy margins of the lake. The shrubbery of the lakeshore is alive with the songs of warblers, vireos, and a great many others in spring. It's also home to a herd of California bighorn sheep, as well as deer and smaller animals such as beavers, muskrats, and bats, snakes, and painted turtles.

There is a Canadian Wildlife Service Sanctuary adjacent to the lake, and a provincial park with nine campsites. It's a good place to quietly paddle at dawn, when the wildlife is most active and the water is usually mirror calm.

Take Highway 97 from Oliver north for sixteen kilometres to a parking lot for the lake.

COUGAR CANYON

• **Feature:** Canyon • **Usual Access:** Day hike • **Time Required:** Half day from Vernon • **Nearest Highway:** Highway 97 • **Best Time To Visit:** Year round • **Maps:** Outdoor Recreation Council - #12 North Okanagan Region 1:100,000

COUGAR CANYON is a seven-kilometre-long gully one kilometre east of Kalamalka Lake in the Okanagan Valley. The canyon floor has a string of tiny ponds, habitat for an amazing diversity of wildlife. Deer, rattlesnakes, bats, and birds from mallards to canyon wrens are found along with wildflowers in spring.

The entire hike to the south end of the canyon rim is nine kilometres one way, so be sure to turn back when you begin to feel tired. It is especially dry and hot in summer, so take a sun hat, sunscreen, water, and carry binoculars for closer looks at the canyon floor.

Because of the canyon's status as a 550-hectare ecological reserve, no disturbing activities are allowed. Throwing rocks from the rim, mountain biking (although this is allowed along the rim), and camping are taboo here.

A trip to Cougar Canyon makes a nice outing from Vernon, especially in early spring when it is cool. From Vernon, take Kalamalka Road east, turning right on Coldstream Road then on to Cosen's Bay Road. Follow this road into Kalamalka Lake Provincial Park and continue to Cosen's Bay parking lot. From the Cosen's Bay trail head, at the end of the parking lot, follow the trail leading to Cosen's Bay. Just after crossing under the power line, the Cougar Canyon trail branches left, continuing under the powerline all the way to the canyon. Once the canyon is reached, the trail follows the northwest rim.

KALAMALKA LAKE

• **Feature:** Beautifully-coloured lake • **Usual Access:** Roadside views • **Time Required:** Half day from Vernon • **Nearest Highway:** Highway 97 • **Best Time To Visit:** Year round • **Maps:** Outdoor Recreation Council - #12 North Okanagan Region 1:100,000

KALAMALKA LAKE is the most colourful of the lakes found in the Okanagan Valley. Named after an Indian who lived at the head of the lake, it's often referred to as "The Lake of a Thousand Colours." Sandy areas at the bottom, at various depths, cause wonderful curving patterns of lighter green hues in the emerald waters. There are spectacular wildflower displays of aridland species around the shore, especially in late spring and summer. The city of Vernon is located at its northern end, making access easy. Kalamalka Lake Provincial Park has trails to viewpoints and good areas for picnicking.

There is an excellent roadside viewpoint eight kilometres north of Oyama on Highway 97, high above the western shore. For closer views, from Vernon, take Kalamalka Road east, turning right on Coldstream Road then proceeding to Cosen's Bay Road. Follow this road into Kalamalka Lake Provincial Park and continue to Cosen's Bay parking lot. This is a good place for picnics and wildflowers. Watch and listen for rattlesnakes.

SPECTRUM FALLS

• **Feature:** Waterfall • **Usual Access:** Roadside • **Time Required:** Day trip • **Nearest Highway:** Highway 6 • **Best Time To Visit:** June to September • **Maps:** NTS 1:50,000 82I/08

SCENIC SPECTRUM FALLS, twelve kilometres outside the western boundary of Monashee Provincial Park, lie in the Monashee Mountains, a rugged range, where the forests are dense and the terrain very steep. Hiking is rather tedious and unrewarding until the higher elevations are reached, and the magnificent alpine scenery is revealed. This area is easily explored on backpacking trips as there are ten wilderness campsites, well set up with picnic tables and toilets at each. For many, the hike through the forest is well worth the trip. Wildlife, from grizzly bears, caribou, and mountain goats, to squirrels, deer mice, and pikas is abundant.

From Vernon take Highway 6 east, seventy-five kilometres to Cherryville, where Sugar Lake Road leads north for forty-eight kilometres. Take the turnoff east and go three kilometres to the Spectrum Trail parking lot, just above the falls.

IDAHO PEAK MEADOWS

• **Feature:** Alpine meadows • **Usual Access:** Four-wheel-drive road and optional day hike • **Time Required:** Half day from New Denver • **Nearest Highway:** Highway 31A • **Best Time To Visit:** Late July to early August • **Maps:** NTS 1:50,000 82F/14; BC Forest Service Recreation Sites - Lower Arrow & Kootenay Lake Area

HIGH ABOVE THE SLOCAN Valley in the southern Selkirk Mountains, Idaho Peak Meadows are considered by many as the best in British Columbia for wildflowers. A four-wheel-drive road leads to a small pass just below the round-ed summit of Idaho Peak. Views from the pass are good, and there are fine wildflower displays around the parking area. The highlight is the summit, reached by hiking an easy trail to a forestry lookout on the mountaintop, where pano-ramas and wildflowers are unparalleled. There is a com-manding view of Kokanee Glacier Park and Slocan Lake, with the Valhalla Ranges backdropping the flowered slopes of Idaho Peak. This is a natural "must see" for visitors to the New Denver area in late July or early August.

From the town of New Denver take Highway 31A for seven kilometres east to the turnoff for Sandon, a mining ghost town. Turn south and go five kilometres to the old town-site. Check at the local Infocentre about road conditions to the meadows and the state of the flower bloom.

From the Infocentre take the four-wheel-drive road eleven kilometres to its end in a small pass. From the parking lot a trail running west climbs steeply through meadow slopes of wildflowers, ending at the forestry lookout. The hike up takes about an hour. Good walking shoes and drinking water are required. With four-wheel-drive access and low visita-tion, these meadows are particularly appealing.

The profusion of blooms is incredible at the right time of year, usually late July through early August, but this varies from year to year depending on snowpack and recent weather. By the time the road is snow free to the top, the first bloom wave is often finished. If visiting early in the flowering season, you may hit that special time when the first bloom wave is in progress on the north side of the nar-row ridge, and the second wave is underway on the south slope just a few metres away.

First wave colours are subtle, pale cream western ane-mones, yellow avalanche lilies, and white spring beauties predominating. The second wave is showier, with red and yellow columbines, purple lupines, and red, orange, and pink paintbrush carpeting the slopes.

Campgrounds and other services are available in New Denver.

THE VALHALLAS

• **Feature:** Mountain scenery • **Usual Access:** Day hike, boat required • **Time Required:** Full day from Nelson • **Nearest Highway:** Highway 6 • **Best Time To Visit:** Late July to early September • **Maps:** NTS 1:50,000 82F/13; BC Forest Service Recreation Sites - Lower Arrow & Kootenay Lake Area

ON THE WEST SIDE of Slocan Lake in the West Kootenay, the towering Valhalla Ranges of the Selkirk Mountains rise above dense forests, turquoise alpine tarns, and riotously-hued alpine meadows, providing some of the most dramatic alpine scenery in B.C. In 1983, 49,200 hectares of this wilderness were set aside as Valhalla Provincial Park. Few visitors to Kootenay country see this magnificence, due to the difficulty in getting there. Rough trails follow major drainages, beginning at various points along the twenty-eight kilometres of western shore on Slocan Lake. With no roads to these lakeside trail heads, however, only travellers with boats can reach the trails.

The most popular trail for a day hike, offering a variety of natural highlights, is the Nemo Creek Trail. From Slocan cross the lake to Nemo Creek. Just north of the creek, the seven-kilometre trail leads along the lakeshore to the "rock castles" formation and Nemo Falls.

There is an alternative, for those without boats, but with four-wheel-drive vehicles. In dry conditions the Drinnon Pass area can be reached from the end of a logging road. From Slocan follow the Little Slocan River Road to Passmore-Hoder Creek junction, continue up Hoder Creek 18.5

kilometres to Hoder-Drinnon Creek junction. At the end of this road up a short spur is a parking lot for the trail to Drinnon Pass. The lakes in this area are scenic and lightly visited. From a base here, there are options for exploring the higher country of this fabulous park, still largely undiscovered by the backpacking crowd.

The Drinnon Pass Trail is 3.5 kilometres, with a 435-metre elevation gain. It takes about two hours. Hikers can continue another 2.2 kilometres, gaining 225 metres in elevation, to Gwillim Lakes. The strength of the party, weather conditions, and time should be considered before continuing if you're doing this as a day hike. Don't get caught in the dark.

This trail provides access for more ambitious excursions in the Valhallas, including a high traverse along the western boundary, or a trip into Mulvey Basin. Contact BC Parks before travelling these routes. Trips in this area should be carefully planned as there are no services. All parties must be properly equipped and self sufficient.

KOKANEE GLACIER

• **Feature:** Glacier and alpine area • **Usual Access:** Backpack • **Time Required:** Overnight • **Nearest Highway:** Highway 3A • **Best Time To Visit:** Year round • **Maps:** NTS 1:50,000 82F/11; BC Parks brochure - Kokanee Glacier

KOKANEE GLACIER is the predominant feature of a high alpine plateau with rugged peaks, glaciers, meadows, waterfalls, and more than thirty lakes. In the Selkirk Mountains northwest of Nelson, for decades it has been a favoured destination for mountaineers and hikers in the West Kootenay, and justifiably so. It is easily accessible to backpackers during summer, and is becoming increasingly popular as a winter destination for back-country skiers, who go there by helicopter.

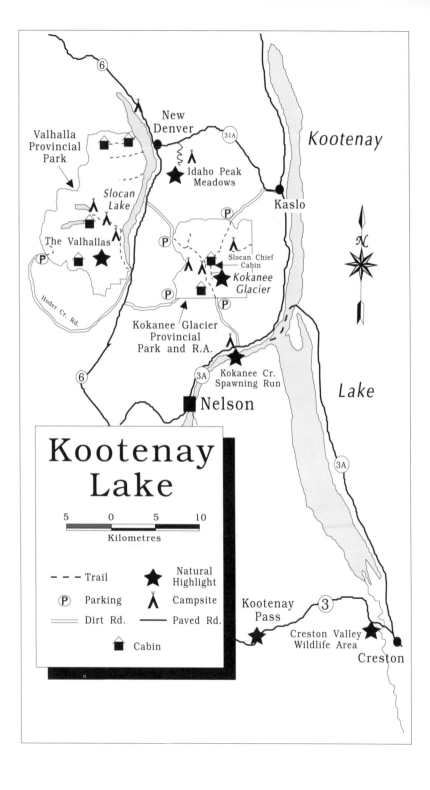

6

New
Denver

Valhalla
Provincial
Park

31A

Kootenay

Idaho Peak
Meadows

*Slocan
Lake*

Kaslo

P

The Valhallas

P

P

P

Slocan Chief
Cabin

*Kokanee
Glacier*

P

Hoder Cr. Rd.

Kokanee Glacier
Provincial
Park and R.A.

P

N

6

3A

Kokanee Cr.
Spawning Run

■ Nelson

Lake

3A

Kootenay
Lake

5	0	5	10
Kilometres

- - - Trail   ★ Natural
Highlight

Ⓟ Parking   ⋀ Campsite

═══ Dirt Rd.   ─── Paved Rd.

⬡ Cabin

Kootenay
Pass

3

Creston Valley
Wildlife Area

Creston

The 32,137-hectare Kokanee Glacier Provincial Park is pure wilderness amid twenty-six-hundred-metre mountains. There are maintained hikers' cabins, outback campsites, and self-guided nature trails. From base camps you can take any number of day hikes to the heart of the park.

From Nelson take Highway 3A for twenty-one kilometres east, to Kokanee Creek Provincial Park. Follow the park signs sixteen kilometres up a rough road to the Gibsons Lake parking lot, the trail head for Kokanee Glacier. From here hike ten kilometres to Slocan Chief Cabin.

From Kaslo take Highway 31A north for five kilometres, then a gravel road for twenty-four kilometres to Joker Millsite. From here hike five kilometres to Slocan Chief Cabin. This cabin sleeps up to twenty people and is almost a hundred years old. It's rustic, but a good place to stay. There is a nightly fee per person, payable to a ranger who comes around to collect. Accommodation here in summer is on a first-come-first-served basis. For reservations, required during winter, call BC Parks in Nelson.

Though picturesque, all glaciers are dangerous. Ice blocks fall from them unexpectedly; avalanches slide from their slopes; crevasses lie agape. Don't go on them unless you have a self-rescue system and are equipped with mountaineering gear, such as crampons, rope, and ice axes.

KOKANEE CREEK

- **Feature:** Spawning kokanee • **Usual Access:** Roadside
- **Time Required:** Half day from Nelson • **Nearest Highway:** Highway 3A • **Best Time To Visit:** August to September • **Maps:** BC Parks brochure - Kokanee Creek

EACH YEAR THOUSANDS of kokanee return to spawn in Kokanee Creek, on the western shore of Kootenay Lake. The spectacle is so significant as a natural event, that the area around the creek mouth is protected as part of Kokanee Creek Provincial Park. Excellent facilities enhance the viewing of the spawning run. Trails run through the moist forests adjacent to the creek; there are camping and nature interpretive programs. Seeing hundreds of bright crimson fish, in a sundappled pool, with huge cedars towering over the whole scene, is an inspiring experience. It is an accessible event, close to the picturesque town of Nelson, at the south end of the lake.

Kokanee are landlocked sockeye salmon, blocked from the sea by natural events, such as rock slides, or by man-made impediments like dams. Kokanee is an Indian word meaning "red fish." Their heads turn green, and their bodies become bright red, as they come to Kokanee Creek to complete their life cycles.

Exhibits and park interpreters provide information about the fish and their habits. Guided walks are conducted daily from August through September, or visitors may wander the creekside trails on their own.

There is a total of 112 sites in two park campgrounds, as well as private campgrounds and other services in Nelson.

This area is also famous for its large osprey population. Watch for a large dark brown and white raptorial bird diving headlong into the water, after hovering above an unwary victim. They carry away surprisingly large fish to nests atop snags or utility poles. Almost extirpated by insecticides in the food chain, they now thrive in the Kokanee Creek area.

From Nelson travel twenty-one kilometres east on Highway 3A to the park entrance.

KOOTENAY PASS

• **Feature:** Woodland caribou and alpine hiking • **Usual Access:** Roadside • **Time Required:** Day trip from Salmo • **Nearest Highway:** Highway 3 • **Best Time To Visit:** July to September • **Maps:** NTS 1:50,000 82F/03

KOOTENAY PASS is an accessible alpine area on the migration route of the woodland caribou. A herd of about thirty
is sometimes seen in this area of the Selkirk Mountains,
thirty-four kilometres west of Creston. The highest paved
road in Canada, at an elevation of 1,774 metres, runs through
the pass. Because of the high elevation, the terrain is almost
treeless, making attractive hiking country with routes along
the tops of ridges. Numerous species of tiny alpine plants,
and miles of unobstructed views reward hikers on the long
rocky ridges.

Kootenay Pass is part of the 1,133-hectare Stagleap Provincial Park. A visitors' centre, with interesting natural history
displays about the area, is located at the west end of Bridal
Lake, beside the highway, with a good picnic area. There
is no camping, but the proximity to the city of Creston makes
it a good choice for day hiking.

Take Highway 3 west from Salmo, for 36.5 kilometres to
a picnic area beside Bridal Lake. There are short walking
trails by the lake, but the best hiking is from the pass itself,
directly into the alpine where hikers can choose their own
routes. Know where you are, and where you need to go,
and keep a watch on the weather. Everything looks the same
when the cloud rolls in.

A special plant found on the shore of Bridal Lake is beargrass, uncommon in the province and quite unusual. Its
1.5-metre-high stalks are crowned with a clublike mass of
tiny white aromatic flowers. This plant blooms as seldom
as once a decade, and only when conditions are just right.

A note of caution: this area undergoes an extensive winter
avalanche-control program. A few projectiles used to explo-
sively release slides before they become major threats invariably do not detonate: hikers should report any to the
park headquarters.

Beargrass in Kootenay Pass.

CRESTON VALLEY WILDLIFE MANAGEMENT AREA

• **Feature:** Marsh wildlife • **Usual Access:** Roadside viewing, short walks, canoe day trips • **Time Required:** Half day from Creston • **Nearest Highway:** Highway 3 • **Best Time To Visit:** May, June and October • **Maps:** Creston Valley Wildlife Management Area — Trail Map

THE CRESTON VALLEY Wildlife Area is a 17,000-hectare wetland adjacent to the Kootenay River. It supports a great variety of wildlife from fourteen-gram rufous hummingbirds, to five-hundred-kilogram elk. The area is managed with a system of dikes and pumps to adjust water levels in the marsh. The Creston Valley Wildlife Management Area is a fine example of what cooperative effort between government and private organizations can achieve.

The area is a beehive of activity in spring, when nesting season is in full swing. More than 250 bird species have been

Creston Valley Wildlife Management Area.

recorded here. Of major significance is the highest concentration of breeding ospreys in Canada, the largest colony of black terns in the province, and the only B.C. colony of Forster's terns. In addition, there are whitetail deer, black bears, otters, moose, and more.

The best way to learn about the area is to visit the interpretive centre which houses natural history displays, a library, and theatre. Binoculars, spotting scopes, field guides, and canoes can be borrowed here. Interpreters are on hand to assist visitors and to lead guided canoe trips through the marshes. Boardwalks lead short distances from the centre to good viewing spots, highlighted by an observation tower for views of the whole area. Trail maps and species lists for different parts of the marsh are available. There is no admission fee, but there is a donations box.

To reach the interpretive centre from Creston, take Highway 3 west for ten kilometres, turn south (left) onto the management area road then go one kilometre to the parking lot.

The Summit Creek Campground, for tents and vehicles, is two kilometres west of the management area road, on the north side of Highway 3, an excellent base for exploring nearby. Elk and whitetail deer are common in the meadows adjacent to the campground, especially in early morning and dusk. From here you can walk miles of trails and dikes.

Mount Assiniboine seen from Citadel Pass.

Rocky Mountains

The mountains in the extreme southeast corner of B.C. are the starting point of one of the province's most unusual geographic features — the Rocky Mountain Trench. This deep valley runs a total of sixteen hundred kilometres along the western side of the Rockies, separating Canada's most famous mountains from the Purcell Range to the west. The Columbia River begins here and winds through the region and down into the United States.

The combination of dramatic topography and running meltwater brings a stunning array of natural highlights to this region. There are spectacular rock towers, pristine alpine lakes, hot springs, and miles of mountain meadows. Many of this region's features are directly accessible from the road, or just a few steps from roadside parking lots. This region alone could provide natural highlights for ten books.

Highways 1, 3, and 93 penetrate this area and there are two border crossings from the U.S., at Kingsgate, Idaho, and Roosville, Montana.

The natural richness of the region is exhibited in the large parks that have been established. Two national parks, Yoho and Kootenay are located along the Trans-Canada Highway and Highway 95. Mount Assiniboine Provincial Park, featuring the sixth-highest peak in the Canadian Rockies, abuts Banff National Park and the Alberta border. It is acessible by foot, horseback, or helicopter only. Equally scenic, but enjoying far less protected status, are Bugaboo Alpine Recre-

Rocky Mountains

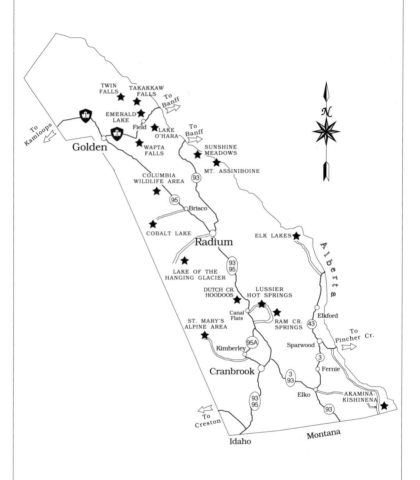

TWIN FALLS

TAKAKKAW FALLS

To Banff

EMERALD LAKE

Field

LAKE O'HARA

To Banff

Golden

WAPTA FALLS

SUNSHINE MEADOWS

MT. ASSINIBOINE

93

COLUMBIA WILDLIFE AREA

95

Brisco

COBALT LAKE

Radium

ELK LAKES

93 95

LAKE OF THE HANGING GLACIER

DUTCH CR. HOODOOS

LUSSIER HOT SPRINGS

Canal Flats

Elkford

ST. MARY'S ALPINE AREA

RAM CR. SPRINGS

43

To Pincher Cr.

Kimberley

95A

Sparwood

3

Cranbrook

3 93

Fernie

93 95

Elko

AKAMINA KISHINENA

To Creston

93

Idaho

Montana

Vancouver

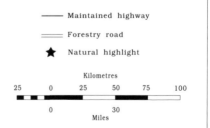

Maintained highway

Forestry road

Natural highlight

Kilometres

25 0 25 50 75 100

0   30

Miles

ation Area (mining and logging permitted) and the Purcell Wilderness Conservancy (protected until we decide to log or mine it). Both are accessible via logging roads from Radium and offer high-quality wilderness recreation.

This region is well known on an international scale as excellent wildlife habitat. More than half of all B.C. bird species nest in this region. The Akamina-Kishinena area, in the extreme southeast corner of the region (and the province), is prime grizzly habitat for the small number of Rocky Mountain grizzlies remaining. Just north of there, Premier Ridge has been designated by the United Nations as site of the most valuable ungulate populations outside of Africa's Serengeti Plains. Visitors who travel this region can see deer, elk, bears, and more.

When coming to the Rocky Mountain region, be prepared for all weather conditions. Hot, cold, wet, dry, this region covers it all. Weather is localized, and therefore fairly unpredictable; summers are usually hot and relatively dry but as you head uphill, it cools off quickly. It can snow in the mountains during any month of the year. Dress in layers so you can remove or add as conditions change. You may be sweating uphill on a hot summer's day but upon reaching that lovely alpine lake, lessened physical activity and higher elevation will get you cold fast. Use sunscreen, sun hats, carry water bottles and rain gear, and don't forget the insect repellent. Those beautiful alpine meadows you see in all the tourism brochures are usually very buggy.

ELK LAKES

• **Feature:** Alpine lake scenery • **Usual Access:** Day hikes and backpacking • **Time Required:** Weekend from Fernie • **Nearest Highway:** Highway 43 • **Best Time To Visit:** July to September • **Maps:** NTS 1:50,000 82J/06,11; B.C. Forest Service Recreation Sites - southeastern

THESE TWO PRETTY mountain-rimmed lakes, named because of the numerous elk once found in the area, are the centrepiece of the 17,325-hectare Elk Lakes Provincial Park and Recreation Area. Excellent day hiking from Lower Elk Lake includes outstanding alpine scenery, towering peaks, waterfalls, meadows, and glaciers. The rugged mountain peaks are part of the Rocky Mountain Front Ranges, known as the French Military Group, named for World War One French Military Officers. It is a little out of the way — just what many people want.

Getting to the lakes on bumpy backroads during spring runoffs and rainy spells when conditions are variable can be difficult. Make a pre-trip check with the Travel Infocentre in Elkford. The area is reached from the southeastern B.C. town of Fernie by driving thirty-two kilometres to Sparwood on Highway 3, then taking Highway 43 north for thirty-five kilometres to Elkford. From Elkford follow the Westside Road to the Elk River crossing. After crossing the river, follow the Kananaskis Power line road for forty-three kilometres northeast to park headquarters. Although this gravel road has been improved in recent years, it is still rough and low clearance vehicles should not attempt it. Remember, this is a wilderness area with no facilities: be prepared to make your own repairs.

The park is also accessible from Alberta's Peter Lougheed Provincial Park by hiking over Elk Pass to Upper Elk Lake. This route is seven kilometres from the trail head to the Petain Campsite near Upper Elk Lake.

An exceptionally beautiful trail providing a fine taste of the area runs from Lower Elk Lake to Upper Elk Lake and beyond to Petain Creek Falls. It is an eight-kilometre one-way trip through meadows, subalpine forests, along the lakeshore of Upper Elk Lake, and over gravelly open outwash plains in the vicinity of Petain Falls. The elevation gain is about two hundred metres and should require about two to three hours to the falls.

There are a few campsites with vehicle access near the park headquarters, and other walk-in campsites at Lower Elk Lake, Petain Creek, and the far western end of Upper Elk Lake. These are the only areas where camping is allowed in the park. Nearby, however, are six B.C. Forest Service campsites at various locations along the road between the Elk River crossing and the park entrance. These are indicated on the B.C. Forest Service map for southeastern B.C. Campers are encouraged to use lightweight mountain stoves in the park rather than deplete the minimal deadwood supply. Cutting trees is prohibited.

Remember to travel prepared even on day hikes. Extra food, clothing for wet and cold weather, a firestarter kit, first aid kit (including bug dope), and at least a BC Parks brochure map, but preferably a compass, topographic map of the area, and the skill to use them.

AKAMINA-KISHINENA RECREATION AREA

• **Feature:** Remote wilderness • **Usual Access:** Logging roads and rough trails • **Time Required:** Weekend from Sparwood • **Nearest Highway:** Highway 3/93 • **Best Time To Visit:** May to September • **Maps:** NTS 1:50,000 82/G01; B.C. Forest Service Recreation Sites - southeastern

THE AKAMINA-KISHINENA area is in extreme southeastern B.C., bordering on the United States and Alberta. It is one of the richest big-game regions in North America. Wedged up against the western slope of the Rockies, it harbours populations of black bears, moose, elk, deer, and a large population of grizzly bears. Usual access is via logging roads into the Akamina-Kishinena Recreation Area. In the Kootenay Indian dialect Akamina means mountain pass. Kishinena has some obscure connection with balsam fir.

From Sparwood on Highway 3 drive south through Corbin to Flathead, near the U.S. border. The area to the east is the recreation area. There are some primitive trails near Kishinena Creek, and B.C. Forest Service campsites at Proctor Lake, Harvey, and Sage creeks. This is an extremely remote wilderness with no services: all travellers should be experienced and well prepared. Consult the local B.C. Forest Service office or the Travel Infocentre in Sparwood for the latest access routes and road conditions, and pick up a Forest Service map before going into the area.

Good bear-country camping practices and common sense are in order here.

ST. MARY'S ALPINE

• **Feature:** Alpine wilderness • **Usual Access:** Backpack
• **Time Required:** Three to seven days • **Nearest Highway:** Highway 95A or Highway 3A • **Best Time To Visit:** July to late September • **Maps:** NTS 1:50,000 82F/16

ST. MARY'S ALPINE Provincial Park is a 9,146-hectare wilderness high in the Purcell Mountains of southeastern B.C. This is a land of superb alpine splendour, with more than twenty-nine small lakes, caribou, waterfalls, dramatic rock walls, and alpine larches that turn golden in autumn. Back-country travellers who are especially fond of remote alpine areas will be in their element, finding their way from one scenic treasure to another. With no development here, the sense of discovery is everpresent. There are no designated campsites, and trails are more or less route-finding exercises. Visitors should be experienced, hardy, skilled with a map and well-acquainted with wilderness ethics. The observant traveller may see mountain goats, grizzlies, and mountain caribou.

Access is via logging roads, requiring a four-wheel-drive

vehicle. From Kimberley on Highway 95 travel south to Marysville. At the south end of town take the St. Mary's Lake gravel road to St. Mary's Alpine Provincial Park for forty-five kilometres north to the park. The rough, steep, forestry trail to Jurek Lake also leads to the park. The southeastern B.C. Forest Service Recreation map shows logging roads into the area. It's available at Travel Infocentres in Radium and Invermere.

LUSSIER HOT SPRINGS

• **Feature:** Riverside hot springs • **Usual Access:** Roadside, short walk down steep stairs • **Time Required:** Half-hour from Canal Flats • **Nearest Highway:** Highway 23 • **Best Time To Visit:** All year, dependent on road conditions • **Maps:** BC Parks brochure - Whiteswan Lake; B.C. Forest Service Recreation Sites - southeastern

THESE SEMI-PRIMITIVE HOT SPRINGS are in Whiteswan Lake Provincial Park, where the Lussier River flows out of the Kootenay Ranges of the Rocky Mountains. Beside the river are three small pools of comfortably hot water — about 43 degrees Celsius — close enough to the icy river for quick cooling-off dips.

This area is in the Rocky Mountain Trench, a region famed for its many developed commercial hot springs resorts. Lussier Hot Springs, being undeveloped, are a pleasant alternative, a more relaxing natural experience. While soaking, bathers have views of mountains and riverside forests, with the soothing sound of the river rushing just a few metres away. Its beautiful setting, easy accessibility, and nearby campsite, make it a popular spot.

Take Highway 93/95, and 4.5 kilometres south of Canal Flats, turn east onto Whiteswan Lake Road, a narrow, rough gravel road used by huge logging and ore trucks: use caution.

Lussier Hot Springs near Radium.

RVs and pickup campers do drive this road and it's usually passable for passenger cars. Continue climbing for 17.8 kilometres to a sign indicating the entrance to the park. The springs are just beyond the entrance on the right. A large sign indicates the top of the stairs. A path leads down from the covered stairway entrance, sixty metres to the pools and river.

The top pool is in a small, square wooden enclosure, suitable for three to five people. The second pool, made deeper by a makeshift boulder dam, holds about ten people. The lowest pool, inundated by the river during high water, has a capacity of fifteen people.

There is a primitive campsite by the springs, and several others farther up the road at Whiteswan Lake. The nearest services are in Canal Flats.

RAM CREEK WARM SPRINGS

• **Feature:** Warm springs • **Usual Access:** Rough one-hundred-metre trail • **Time Required:** One hour from Canal Flats • **Nearest Highway:** Highway 93/95 • **Best Time To Visit:** All year • **Maps:** BC Parks brochure - Top Of The World

THESE SPRINGS ARE WARM — about 35 degrees Celsius — not hot. They are, however, beautifully situated above a forested valley on the east side of the Rocky Mountain Trench, between Canal Flats and Cranbrook. Bathers have built a boulder dam to deepen the waters, forming quite a large pool, capable of holding twenty friendly people at a time. This makes a good summer day outing from Radium.

From Radium travel south seventy-two kilometres to Canal Flats. From here travel Highway 93/95, south for twenty-seven kilometres to Premier Lake Road, then head east 9.5 kilometres passing the turnoff for Premier Lake to where the road forks. Here take main Sheep Creek Road north, crossing Lussier River, then continue 11.5 kilometres. Park here where the road curves right and goes uphill. A path leads up the hill to the springs.

The springs are in an ecological reserve so camping is not allowed. There are campsites at Premier Lake and Whiteswan Lake.

Dutch Creek Hoodoos between Invermere and Canal Flats.

DUTCH CREEK HOODOOS

- **Feature:** Eroded cliff formation • **Usual Access:** Roadside
- **Time Required:** One hour from Radium • **Nearest Highway:** Highway 95 • **Best Time To Visit:** Year-round • **Maps:** Outdoor Recreation Council - Windermere Region 1:100,000

THE DUTCH CREEK hoodoos are unusual towers and fin-like formations in the hard conglomerate rock above the south end of Columbia Lake, near Invermere. According to Indian legend a big fish tried to make it up the Rocky Mountain Trench via the Kootenay and the Columbia rivers, but died at Dutch Creek. The vertical hoodoos are its bones. From the south they are visible for quite a distance as a light-coloured band above the highway, near where Dutch Creek enters the lake. The seventy-metre-high hoodoo cliff stretches half a kilometre along the north side of Highway 95 at the Dutch Creek bridge.

Fortunately the hoodoos are easy to see from the road and, in fact, many drivers don't even slow down. A visit is a good two-hour drive from Radium.

The hoodoo formation is reached from Radium by driving south on Highway 95 for fifty-eight kilometres to the Dutch Creek bridge. Approaching from the south, they are 13.5 kilometres north of Canal Flats. There are small pulloff spots near the bridge over Dutch Creek but a safer place to stop is a cleared area reached by a logging road which heads north off the highway at the east end of the bridge. Use caution turning off here as there may be logging equipment or vehicles in the area.

The pine forest at the base of the cliffs is a good place to listen for owls, a pleasant spot to stretch the legs for a few minutes. Wild roses and saskatoons bloom here in spring. Deer, sheep, and moose may be seen at dusk or in early morning. Resist the urge to climb among the hoodoos. Large rocks fall from the formations and the slopes do not provide good footing.

LAKE OF THE HANGING GLACIER

• **Feature:** Alpine lake • **Usual Access:** Day hike • **Time Required:** Full day • **Nearest Highway:** Highway 95 • **Best Time To Visit:** July to August • **Maps:** NTS 1:50,000 82K/07; Outdoor Recreation Council - Windermere Area 1:100,000; B.C. Forest Service Recreation Sites - southeastern

---

LAKE OF THE HANGING GLACIER is a pristine lake high in the Purcell Mountains, west of the Rocky Mountain Trench. A highly scenic area, it features a fifty-metre-high glacier tongue calving ice blocks into the turquoise waters of the lake. Around the lake are alpine meadows with spectacular displays in mid to late summer of mountain flowers such as Indian paintbrush, lupine, and arnicas. The setting is a classic — high steep mountains with crystal blue glaciers on their flanks, mirrored on the lake surface. It is best visited in late summer since it lies at 2,581 metres above sea level: summer comes late here. A two-hundred-metre-long stretch of rapids exits at the south end of the lake.

Visitors should be prepared for wintry weather at any time of year and be in good physical condition to handle the altitude.

There's lots here for the day hiker, but a backpacking journey is the best way to fully appreciate the area. There are places begging to be explored. Glacier Dome and close up views of the glacier at the far end of the lake are both worthwhile walks from a base camp in the larch forest below the lake.

As a day trip, over a third of the journey is spent driving logging roads to and from the trail head. Drive west from Radium on the Horsethief Creek forestry road. Rugged two-wheel-drive vehicles often make this trip but may not be able to ford a creek two kilometres from the Lake of the Hanging Glacier trail head. A four-wheel-drive vehicle is recommended. Take this road fifty-six kilometres to the end.

The five-kilometre trail is unmarked at the beginning but is easy to find, heading uphill on the north side of the parking lot. After a half hour of hiking take a fork in the trail to the left — the right is for horses — and cross the raging waters of the creek on an aluminum bridge. The uphill trail follows the creek until it breaks into open larch forest and flower meadows, about a kilometre from the lake. There is good camping in a meadow just before the lake, offering more shelter from icy winds than the campsite right beside the lake. The trail can be done as a day hike of about five to six hours return from the parking lot. The road takes one to two hours one way from Radium so allow a full day for this trip.

Check locally before setting out since road conditions and routes may change without notice. There are guided hiking tours operated from Radium and heli-hiking possibilities as well.

COBALT LAKE

• **Feature:** Scenic alpine lake • **Usual Access:** Logging roads then day hike • **Time Required:** Full day from Radium • **Nearest Highway:** Highway 95 • **Best Time To Visit:** July to September • **Maps:** NTS 1:50,000 82K/15; B.C. Forest Service Recreation Sites - Radium Area; Outdoor Recreation Council - Windermere Region 1:100,000

COBALT LAKE lies high in the Bugaboo Range of the northern Purcell Mountains, west of the Rocky Mountain Trench. Deep blue as the name implies, it is set magnificently against a backdrop of huge granite towers. The surrounding slopes are cloaked in alpine wildflowers in late July and early August, providing photographers and artists with classic mountain compositions.

Cobalt Lake is situated within Bugaboo Glacier Provincial Park and Alpine Recreation Area, west of the resort town of Radium. In one day you can trek to the lake then return for a soothing soak in the hot springs at Radium. Get an early start.

From Radium drive north on Highway 95 for twenty-nine kilometres to Brisco. BC Parks signs mark the turnoff west onto the logging road that continues forty-five kilometres to Bugaboo Glacier Park. Although a good road, its condition varies with the seasons. Check with the Travel Infocentre in Radium before setting out. Once at the recreation area the trail-head parking lot is well marked. Visitors are asked to not use the private parking area of nearby Canadian Mountain Holidays Lodge.

The trail switchbacks steeply through an old burn to a high ridge overlooking the lake and dramatic landscapes beyond. For many, this ridge, reached in one and one half to two hours, is the final destination. Views from here feature the dramatic granite towers of Brenta, Northpost, and Cobalt Lake spires rising above the lake, providing one of the finest landscapes of the region.

The lakeshore is reached by a short easy hike down from the ridge through open meadows. From this perspective there are also excellent views, especially during calm spells when the lake mirrors the surrounding mountains.

The distance from the trail head to the lakeshore is five kilometres. The return route back to the parking lot is along the same trail. The entire hike takes two to three hours.

A good pair of hiking boots and a little determination are needed. Take it seriously, however, as mountain weather is fickle; a perfect sunny day can quickly change into wintery conditions. The peaks around the lake rise to over twenty-nine hundred metres, serving to obscure storm clouds lurking on the other side. Rain gear and extra warm clothing are a must for any trip here.

Hikers wishing to get an early start have the option of staying overnight in a small B.C. Forest Service campsite situated a short way up Bugaboo Creek. It is reached by taking the logging road turnoff south just before Canadian Mountain Holidays Lodge. The campsite is signposted and is just a few minutes up this road.

There are interesting hiking options available for Cobalt Lake visitors. Commercial outfits offer one-day guided hikes to the lake as well as heli-hiking. Check with the Radium Travel Infocentre.

Being largely alpine, this area is extremely fragile: it takes years to recover from damaging human activities. It must be used responsibly if it is to offer prime recreation in the future. In the past, meadows have been trampled and wild-flower populations depleted by visitors gathering bouquets. The blooms are usually wilted and unattractive by the time the hikers get them back to their vehicles. BC Parks is trying to protect and rehabilitate the area. It is illegal to take flowers or other natural things. Hikers should stay on established trails and leave dogs at home. Use a small mountain stove for cooking — campfires are prohibited. To keep water clean, wash dishes or bodies well away from lakes and streams. Following these guidelines will help preserve the naturalness that attracts us in the first place.

Useful information and trail maps are available in the Bugaboo Glacier and Recreation Area, and brochures are available from BC Parks or Travel Infocentres.

COLUMBIA WILDLIFE AREA

• **Feature:** Wetlands wildlife • **Usual Access:** Roadside • **Time Required:** One to three hours from Radium or Golden • **Nearest Highway:** Highway 95 • **Best Time To Visit:** May to June, and October • **Maps:** Outdoor Recreation Council - Windermere Region 1:100,000

THE COLUMBIA WILDLIFE AREA is on a meandering section of the Columbia River and adjacent wetlands between Radium and Golden. Highway 95, connecting these two towns in the Rocky Mountain Trench, parallels the river for one hundred kilometres, providing excellent wildlife viewing. Caused by yearly flooding of the Columbia, the innumerable ponds and marshes provide habitat for vast numbers of migrating and nesting birds.

In a half day from Radium or Golden you should see many interesting species. Canada geese, snow geese, wood ducks, pintails, and shovelers paddle the ponds. Ospreys, eagles, and vultures patrol the skies overhead, while herons fish the shallows. Warblers, flycatchers, and vireos scour the willows and alders lining the waterways. It's especially busy here in spring so bring a bird book and a good pair of binoculars to keep up with the goings on.

Of special significance along the highway is the second-largest nesting colony of great blue herons in western Canada. The rookery of more than three hundred nests, can be seen from the road about 31.5 kilometres north of Radium.

Ponds along the Columbia River.

Between Harrogate and Golden watch for small wooden platforms in the roadside ponds. These provide nesting sites for Canada geese. In early spring the adult can be seen sitting atop the nest, and, in late May and June, leading a flotilla of downy goslings.

The large brown and white hawk commonly seen hovering above the water, before making a spectacular splashing dive, is an osprey. Known as "fish hawks," they have made a dramatic comeback from near extinction. The Columbia River supports one of the highest concentrations of ospreys in Canada. Their huge nests sit on the tops of utility poles and dead snags along the highway.

For a closer look at the wetlands, take a side-trip loop that leaves Highway 95 and heads west from either Brisco or Spillimacheen, continuing on good gravel surface. This "Westside Loop" crosses the Columbia and travels close by the marshes and ponds before returning to the paved highway at either Brisco or Spillimacheen, depending on where you started.

Keep an eye out for birds and other animals in this area. You may be lucky to see deer, moose, or black bears. The best time to visit is early morning or evening in spring or fall.

WAPTA FALLS

• **Feature:** Waterfall • **Usual Access:** Day hike • **Time Required:** Half day from Golden • **Nearest Highway:** Highway 1 (Trans-Canada) • **Best Time To Visit:** May to September

A PLEASANT AND EASY walk through the forest to Wapta Falls, in Yoho National Park, is a nice break from travelling the Trans-Canada Highway. Although Wapta Falls are not among the highest waterfalls in B.C., they are in a wonderful setting and have an interesting form, being wider than they are high. The Kicking Horse River encounters a twenty-metre drop in the riverbed, forming Wapta Falls. A large block of limestone at the bottom of the drop blocks the river and forces the energized water to suddenly divert around it, creating a spectacular display of raging waters.

Wapta is the Stoney Indian word for river, an understatement for the section of river at Wapta Falls.

From the western entrance to Yoho Park travel east on the Trans-Canada for four kilometres, then turn right on a gravel road and go 2.5 kilometres to the parking lot at the Wapta Falls trail head.

The 1.5-kilometre trail to the falls is an easy walk through the forest and occasional clearings. Along the way, especially in spring, you may see grouse, deer, and wildflowers at the edges of the clearings. Of particular interest to flower lovers is the exquisite calypso orchid, one of the most beautiful flowers in B.C. Look in the mossy carpet of the forest adjacent to the trail. Resisting the temptation to pick a few will allow others to enjoy them in future. It is also against the law.

The trail arrives at a viewpoint above the falls. Over the years adventurous types have worn several other pathways down to the river. It is hard on the forest to have these additional unofficial trails, where erosion is a problem: stay on designated trails. These secondary routes are dangerous as the spray from the falls makes them slippery, posing a hazard near the edge of the cliffs above the river.

MOUNT REVELSTOKE MEADOWS

• **Feature:** Alpine meadows • **Usual Access:** Roadside • **Time Required:** One hour from Revelstoke • **Nearest Highway:** Highway 1 (Trans-Canada) • **Best Time To Visit:** Early August • **Maps:** NTS 1:50,000 82M/01, 82N/04

OF ALL THE SPECTACULAR subalpine wildflower meadows in British Columbia, Mount Revelstoke is one of the most easily accessible. The rounded summit has hectares of meadows at their best in late July and early August. A well maintained network of loop trails, requiring fifteen minutes to an hour to complete, radiates from the summit parking lot. Three hundred and sixty degree panoramas keep photographers snapping. Views of the Selkirks, Monashees, and the Columbia River delight visitors to this, the most popular location in Mount Revelstoke National Park. It's a good place to spend an hour or full day wandering the trails or soaking up the nature of the place. Sunsets are unforgettable from this setting, drawing small quiet crowds from the town of Revelstoke, just a half hour away by paved road.

From Revelstoke take the Trans-Canada Highway one kilometre east to Summit Road, then drive twenty-six kilometres to the summit.

ILLECILLEWAET GLACIER

• **Feature:** Glacier • **Usual Access:** Day hike • **Time Required:** Full day from Revelstoke • **Nearest Highway:** Highway 1 (Trans-Canada) • **Best Time To Visit:** June to October • **Maps:** NTS 1:50,000 82N/03

THE ILLECILLEWAET GLACIER looms over the Trans-Canada Highway as the road runs through the valley of the Illecillewaet River. Posing no immediate threat to travellers on the Trans-Canada, this river of ice, in the past, protruded much farther into the valley through which the highway now runs. For almost a hundred years since its discovery it has receded, melting away from the valley floor. Recently, however, it has entered an advancing stage, albeit at an excruciatingly slow pace of a mere ten metres per year. It is possible that one day it will block the highway with tons of ice. The glacier lies just west of Rogers Pass in Glacier National Park.

Illecillewaet is an Okanagan Indian word meaning "big water." This natural attraction is certainly big water even though it is in the solid state. It requires a 4.8-kilometre hike on the Great Glacier Trail to see it up close. From Revelstoke travel east for sixty-seven kilometres on the Trans-Canada to the entrance to Illecillewaet Campground, just west of Rogers Pass. Take the turnoff south and proceed past the campground where there are signs for various trail heads heading out from the campground. The trek to the glacier is a two-to-three-hour uphill grind, a good test for the lungs. This effort is rewarded by tremendous views of the glacier's snout. The long, punishing downhill trek is a good test for the knees. Wear good hiking boots. Carry a day pack with rain gear and extra clothing as it may be cool near the glacier and weather deteriorates quickly in this area.

EMERALD LAKE

• **Feature:** Subalpine lake and mountain scenery • **Usual Access:** Roadside view with optional walk • **Time Required:** One and a half to two hours for the walk • **Nearest Highway:** Highway 1 (Trans-Canada) • **Best Time To Visit:** June to October

SURROUNDED BY THE SHEER faces of Rocky Mountain summits in Yoho National Park, rimmed with cool coniferous forests, it is the type of place brought to mind when one imagines the Rockies. Emerald Lake is one of the main attractions in Yoho Park, attracting photographers and artists from all over the world. Relatively unspoiled, despite the large number of visitors, it is still possible near the beginning or end of the tourist season to walk the trail around the lake without encountering anyone.

Emerald Lake may be seen by taking a ten-minute detour from the Trans-Canada Highway. Travel east on the Trans-Canada from Field, in Yoho Park, for two kilometres to the Emerald Lake turnoff. Go north on the paved Emerald Lake Road for 7.5 kilometres to the lake.

From the east end of the parking lot is a good five-kilometre trail encircling the lake: it takes an hour or two to complete. It is cleared and level, easily done in comfortable walking shoes. In early morning, or just after sunset, when wildlife is most active, you may see moose, especially in the boggy area at the north end of the lake.

Clearings caused by winter avalanches thundering down on the lake become grassy meadows and willow thickets in early spring. Later, in late May and early June, they are covered with millions of yellow avalanche lilies and white spring beauties.

One of the nicest ways to enjoy the lake is by canoe. The water is often glass calm, especially in morning. It can be magical, with loons calling as the first light warms the upper cliffs of Mount Burgess, high above the western shore. Morning mist on the lake, backdropped by the golden light on the summits above is a common scene in fall. Launching areas are near the parking lot and rentals are available at the lodge. No power boats disturb this tranquility: they are not permitted at Emerald Lake.

Although there is no camping at the lake, there is accommodation at the Emerald Lake Lodge and at a nearby hostel or in Yoho Park campgrounds.

LAKE O'HARA

• **Feature:** Scenic alpine area • **Usual Access:** Long hike or bus • **Time Required:** Two to seven days • **Nearest Highway:** Highway 1 (Trans-Canada) • **Best Time To Visit:** July to October • **Maps:** NTS 1:50,000 82N/08

LAKE O'HARA, in Yoho National Park, is yet another classic Rocky Mountain setting. Dozens of small lakes, ranging in colour from turquoise to emerald green to azure blue, lie within easy day hiking range. Most are connected by an

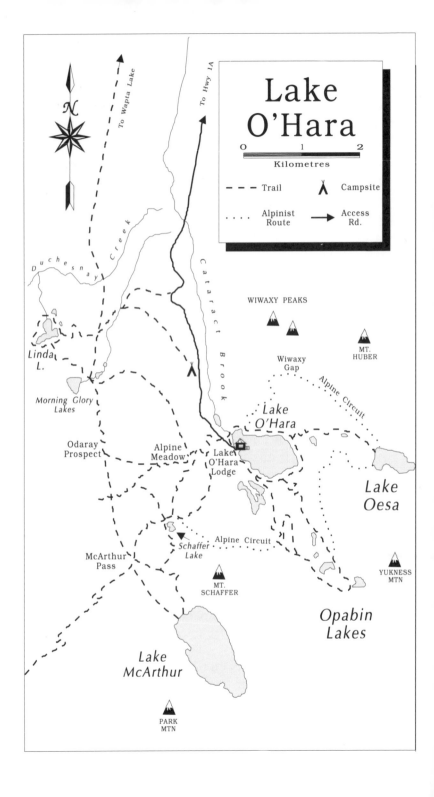

excellent trail network. Larch forests fringe the lakes with gold in the fall, and icy summits encircle this pocket of alpine splendour. Some Rocky Mountain enthusiasts visit Lake O'Hara exclusively, returning year after year, knowing they are seeing the best the Rockies has to offer. It has been described as "What Lake Louise was like before the highway." For the time being it should remain in this unspoiled state as there is no vehicle access except by the Lake O'Hara Lodge bus.

Private vehicle access ends at a parking lot on the old Trans-Canada Highway, now Highway 1A. Visitors take the trail or bus thirteen kilometres up to Lake O'Hara. To reach the parking lot take the Trans-Canada Highway to Field then go east for 13.5 kilometres to the junction with Highway 1A. Take 1A two hundred metres to the parking lot.

Reservations are needed for Lake O'Hara Lodge situated on the lakeshore, and a thirty-site campground five hundred metres before the lake. You also need to book a ride up in the bus. Contact the Canadian Parks Service in Field.

The trail network is well marked and information is available at the park office near the lake. One of the best trails is the Alpine Circuit, a high route of about twelve kilometres encircling the lake and offering views to stun the most jaded alpine traveller.

It begins at the outlet of the lake just a few hundred metres from the lodge or campground. If hiking in a clockwise direction from the outlet of Lake O'Hara, the Wiwaxy Gap Trail branches off to the left after about two hundred metres. It gets the blood pumping in a steep ascent for two kilometres, finally reaching Wiwaxy Gap. The views on both sides of this gap are unparalleled. Mountain goats are often seen here and are usually quite relaxed for photographers. Remember not to approach or feed any of the park wildlife.

Two kilometres farther along, the trail intersects the trail to Lake Oesa. It continues on wide ledges high above Lake O'Hara to kilometre 6.4, where the Opabin Plateau Trail goes

Lake O'Hara from Wiwaxy Gap.

left to Opabin Lake. There are magnificent larch forests here, golden in late September. From Opabin Lake head right following the Opabin West Circuit for 1.6 kilometres, then turn left onto the All Souls' Alpine Route. Travel 1.8 kilometres to another junction where you turn left onto Big Larch Route, which takes you one hundred metres to Schaffer Lake. From here take the McArthur Lake Trail 1.5 kilometres back to the lodge, just a few steps from where you started.

The entire circuit may be done in five to six hours but it usually takes most of the day when allowing for long rest breaks to enjoy the scenery. Take warm clothing and rain gear, with lunch and other essentials for day hiking in the mountains, where weather changes quickly.

TAKAKKAW FALLS

- **Feature:** Third-highest waterfall in British Columbia
- **Usual Access:** Roadside • **Time Required:** Half-hour from Field • **Nearest Highway:** Highway 1 (Trans-Canada)
- **Best Time To Visit:** July to October

TAKAKKAW FALLS live up to their name, derived from a Cree Indian word meaning "magnificent." These are the highest waterfalls in the Rockies at 254 metres. They are easy to get to; practically anyone can visit these falls.

Takakkaw Falls can be reached by a short paved road in Yoho National Park, a half-hour to one-hour side trip from the Trans-Canada Highway. There are great views from the parking lot. Along easy walking trails are views of the falls dropping from the top of the sheer rock face to the Yoho River.

From Field, on the Trans-Canada Highway, go east 3.5 kilometres to the Yoho Valley Road and turn north (left). Drive fifteen kilometres to the falls. This road has sharp s-bends and is unsuitable for large trailers or RVs.

The falls can be seen as you approach the parking lot. For more dramatic views from the banks of the Yoho River, take a two-to-three-minute walk from the parking area. By crossing the river on a footbridge, visitors keen on a closer view can follow a trail leading up to the base of the falls. Long before the base is reached, however, you will be soaked from the spray, so dress accordingly. Take special note that the jumble of boulders near the base of the falls has come from above and new ones come tumbling down from time to time.

One of the best views of the falls is from the Iceline Trail, which starts from a youth hostel a few hundred metres before the falls parking area. The trail begins at the south side of the parking lot, heading steeply uphill through avalanche slopes for ten to fifteen minutes. Because the sun is at your

Takakkaw Falls, highlight of the Yoho Valley.

back here, rainbows appear in the mist of the falls, especially on windy days when the spray is more dispersed.

From this vantage point you can see Daly Glacier, its meltwater dropping in a series of cascades to the edge of a cliff at the top of the waterfall. After pounding into the valley floor, the waters join the Yoho River, flowing through one of the continent's most beautiful areas, the Yoho Valley.

Trailers can be left in the park at Kicking Horse Campground, at the bottom of the Yoho Valley Road. The walk-in campground is beautifully situated five hundred metres from the falls parking lot: many sites have views of the falls. Rickshaw-type carts are available to haul camping gear along the trail so coolers and heavier equipment can be easily carried. It is one of the more pleasant campsites in the Rockies, with no vehicles, within easy reach of trails to the upper Yoho Valley, and continually soothed by the distant rumble of the waterfall.

TWIN FALLS

• **Feature:** Twin cascades • **Usual Access:** Day hike • **Time Required:** Full day from Field • **Nearest Highway:** Highway 1 (Trans-Canada) • **Best Time To Visit:** July to October • **Maps:** NTS 1:50,000 82N/08,09

THESE SIDE-BY-SIDE WATERFALLS drop eighty metres over a limestone precipice within view of a chalet where hikers can put their feet up and enjoy the marvellous view. Twin Falls is just one of the many highlights along the Twin Falls Trail in Yoho National Park. Hikers can visit the falls as a day trip from the Takakkaw Falls area, or as part of a longer backpacking route. Scenery along the way up the Yoho Valley is great.

The trail to Twin Falls starts at the Takakkaw Falls parking lot. From the town of Field on the Trans-Canada Highway head east 3.5 kilometres to the Yoho Valley Road and turn north. Sharp s-bends on this steep road make it impassable to large RVs and trailers which can be left near the Kicking Horse Campground.

Begin this hike by walking the five-hundred-metre trail to the walk-in campground at Takakkaw Falls. Follow the trail (an old road) beyond the walk-in campground and after 2.4 kilometres watch for two cutoffs, first to Angel's Staircase Falls, then, a little farther along the main trail, to Point Lace Falls. Both are attractive falls, especially in early summer — well worth the short side trips.

Continue through the forest to Laughing Falls, at kilometre 4.7, and beyond to kilometre 6.5 and the junction with Yoho Glacier Trail. Take the left fork, which rises steadily to the Twin Falls Chalet at kilometre 8.5.

This is a fairly easy day hike but has some demoralizing uphill sections, most notably, just after a sign indicating 1.6 kilometres to the falls: you realize here that it's going to be an uphill challenge for this final push to the viewpoint. The trail goes a hundred metres past the Twin Falls Chalet to a footbridge across the creek where there is an excellent view of the falls, still high above.

An interesting option to day hiking this route is to make it a backpacking loop. Trails continue past the chalet and circle back via the Yoho Iceline Trail to the youth hostel, just a short walk from the Takakkaw Falls parking lot. This is one of the finest trails in the Rockies for fabulous views. Twin Falls Chalet offers overnight accommodation but reservations are required well in advance.

SUNSHINE MEADOWS

• **Feature:** Alpine meadows on continental divide • **Usual Access:** Day hike • **Time Required:** Full day from Banff or Lake Louise • **Nearest Highway:** Highway 1 (Trans-Canada)

• **Best Time To Visit:** Late July early August • **Maps:** NTS
1:50,000 82J/13; BC Parks brochure - Mt. Assiniboine

THIS VAST ALPINE AREA along the continental divide is
one of the finest areas in Canada to witness the explosive
colours of alpine wildflowers. They seem in a frenzy to complete their growing cycle, to seed in the brief snow-free season. There are loop trails of varying lengths for both the
casual walker and stronger hiker.

Located in Mount Assiniboine Provincial Park, adjacent
to Banff National Park, the alpine scenery here is unforgettable. The classic horn of Mount Assiniboine dominates the
skyline to the south and west; north and east are filled with
the jagged outlines of Banff Park. The best time to see the
flowers varies from year to year, but usually a visit in early
to mid-August will be rewarded with colourful meadow
scenes.

These trails begin at the Sunshine Village Ski Area which,
until recently, was accessible via a gondola from Bourgeau
parking lot. This service was discontinued in 1991 and its
future was undecided. Now it's a six-kilometre uphill hike
to the start of the loop trails. It is well worth it, but unfor-
tunate that some less able walkers are denied the delights
of the area.

To get to the trail head take the Trans-Canada Highway
ten kilometres west of Banff, turning south at the signs for
Sunshine Village. Continue fourteen kilometres to the
Bourgeau parking lot. The gravel road heads uphill behind
the gondola for six kilometres. It isn't the most pleasant hike
in the world, being on a dusty road, but there are some good
views of the mountains back down the valley. It takes only
a couple of hours to get to the meadows above the ski area.

MOUNT ASSINIBOINE

• **Feature:** Sixth-highest peak in Rocky Mountains • **Usual Access:** Backpack or fly-in • **Time Required:** One week • **Nearest Highway:** Highway 95 or Highway 1 (Trans-Canada) • **Best Time To Visit:** July to September • **Maps:** NTS 1:50,000 82J/13; BC Parks brochure - Mt. Assiniboine

MOUNT ASSINIBOINE is the sixth-highest peak in the Rocky Mountains. Its 3,618-metre pyramid rises far above any other summit for miles around, standing out like Switzerland's Matterhorn. Since 1922 it has been the centrepiece of Mount Assiniboine Provincial Park, abutting the southern boundary of Banff National Park in the southern Rockies. It is one of the prime goals in the Rockies for mountaineers.

It rivals Lake O'Hara and Berg Lake as the finest hiking area in the B.C. Rockies. At its base are several pristine lakes. Extensive meadows filled with mid-summer blooms stretch for several kilometres, interrupted here and there with alpine larches that turn golden in the fall. Numerous day hiking routes radiate from the core area around Lake Magog, the largest lake here. Access routes are long but scenic. The area around the base of the mountain is popular, but there is lots of room to get away to more remote areas that still have excellent views of the imposing peak.

The usual methods of access are hiking, horseback, and helicopter. Horse trips require pre-registration through the BC Parks office at Wasa. Helicopters fly into the area on certain days of the week: contact BC Parks. There are several hiking routes into the park around Lake Magog. The two most popular are the Spray Reservoir route and the Sunshine route.

To reach the Spray Reservoir route from Canmore Alberta, travel fifteen kilometres south on the Spray Reservoir Road to the junction of Smith Dorian Highway and West Shore Access Road. Follow West Shore Access Road sixteen kilometres to the dam parking lot. Four-wheel-drive vehicles may continue another five kilometres beyond the parking area.

From the parking area the route goes up Bryant Creek for seventeen kilometres to Assiniboine Pass before arriving at Lake Magog, 3.6 kilometres on the other side of the pass. This will probably take six to seven hours.

To start the Sunshine route take Trans-Canada Highway for ten kilometres west from Banff to the turnoff for Sunshine Village Ski Area and then go south for fourteen kilometres to the Bourgeau parking lot. Hike six kilometres uphill to the ski area. From here the route is via Quartz Ridge, then Citadel Pass and Valley of Rocks. Lake Magog is twenty-seven kilometres, at least eight hours, from the start of the hike.

The Sunshine route is extremely scenic, travelling through open wildflower meadows and rock gardens, past tiny alpine lakes, and in fall, through miles of red alpine foliage and golden larch forests.

Both routes have campsites along the way. Those in Banff National Park must be booked and paid for in advance at Canadian Park Service offices in Banff or Lake Louise. The core area campsites and cabins are available on a first-come-first-served basis. It may be crowded, so arrive equipped to camp out.

Campfires are not allowed in the core area so pack a stove. There are wood stoves in the cabins.

Large animals such as mule deer, black and grizzly bears, moose, elk, and wolves inhabit these mountains along with marmots, coyotes, and other smaller mammals. The growing season is short and intense with snow patches lingering in brilliant wildflower meadows even in late July. Trails are well used and maintained and are usually snow free by August, except on northern exposures at higher elevations.

Storms may bring snow on any day of the year so backpackers should be prepared for all weather conditions. There are park and commercial cabins, known as the Naiset Cabins, near the west shore of Lake Magog.

Easy day hikes from the core area include Og Lake at 5.6 kilometres, Gog Lake at 1.8 kilometres, and Wonder Pass Viewpoint at 5.6 kilometres. A four-kilometre hike to Nub Lake requires moderate stamina. The 4.8-kilometre Mount Cautley and 5.7-kilometre Windy Ridge hikes could be classed as strenuous. From Sunburst Lake there are three moderate hikes — Rock Lake at 11.3 kilometres, Elizabeth Lake at 1.7 kilometres, and Wedgewood Lake at 5.1 kilometres.

If possible, allow for a week in this area. It is scenic on an international scale.

Berg Glacier near Mount Robson.

High Country

The High Country region of east-central B.C. is more diverse than any other. With the Cariboo-Chilcotin on the north, and the Rockies and Okanagan-Kootenay to the south, it has both arid grasslands and wet forests. The Thompson, Columbia, and other major rivers flow through this region; big lakes like Shuswap and Revelstoke are boaters' highways to remote and forested valleys. There are waterfalls, salmon streams, glaciers, and more.

Several highways run through the High Country region; the most frequently travelled are Highways 1 and 5.

With hundreds of lakes, the Rocky Mountain Trench, four mountain ranges plus a summer average temperature ranging from 21 to 32 degrees Celsius, it is little wonder that natural highlight seekers are drawn to this region. They come to see the Rockies' highest Canadian peak, concentrations of waterfalls, lush flower meadows, migrating salmon and endangered scenic grasslands.

Two national parks — Mount Revelstoke and Glacier — are found along the Trans-Canada in the east. Two of the most scenic provincial parks — Wells Gray and Mount Robson — are found in the north along the Yellowhead Highway. Wildlife is plentiful: moose, deer, grizzly and black bears, elk, wolves, mountain goats, geese, swans and hundreds of other bird species may be found.

Activities will dictate your clothing requirements as the weather varies as much as the terrain. Make sure you have

High Country

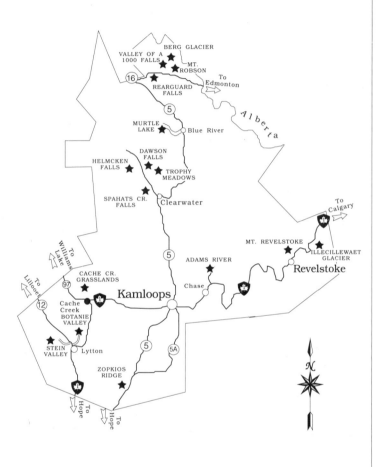

BERG GLACIER
VALLEY OF A
1000 FALLS
MT.
ROBSON
To
Edmonton
16
REARGUARD
FALLS
5
Alberta
MURTLE
LAKE
Blue River
DAWSON
FALLS
HELMCKEN
FALLS
TROPHY
MEADOWS
SPAHATS CR.
FALLS
Clearwater
To
Calgary
5
MT. REVELSTOKE
ADAMS RIVER
ILLECILLEWAET
GLACIER
To
Williams
Lake
Revelstoke
CACHE CR.
GRASSLANDS
97
Kamloops
Chase
To
Lillooet
12
Cache
Creek
BOTANIE
VALLEY
STEIN
VALLEY
Lytton
5
5A
ZOPKIOS
RIDGE
N
To
Hope
To
Hope

Vancouver

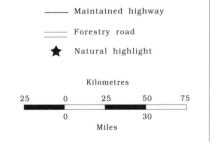

——— Maintained highway

——— Forestry road

★ Natural highlight

Kilometres

25   0   25   50   75

0   30

Miles

good rain gear. Much of the region is in the interior wet belt which, although drier than the coast, can still get a week of rainy weather even in mid-summer. As with the Rocky Mountain region, it gets cooler with altitude here, so bring clothes you can layer according to conditions. Sunscreen and insect repellent are especially important here as many areas of the interior wet belt are major breeding sites for mosquitos. Even in the arid areas mosquitos find places to breed, and there is the added nuisance of horse and deer flies.

Using Kamloops as a base, visitors can explore this region easily on weekend trips or as an extended vacation, perhaps taking a circular route from Kamloops up the Yellowhead to Mount Robson, then south along the Icefields Parkway to Lake Louise, Mount Revelstoke, and back to Kamloops. This trip takes five to seven days depending on how many side trips are taken.

ZOPKIOS RIDGE

• **Feature:** Dramatic rock faces • **Usual Access:** Roadside views • **Time Required:** One hour from Hope • **Nearest Highway:** Highway 5 • **Best Time To Visit:** Year round • **Maps:** NTS 1:50,000 92H/11

THE HUGE GRANITIC SLABS of Zopkios Ridge, beside the Coquihalla Highway between Hope and Merritt, are dramatic year round. After being blasted with fresh winter snow, bare rock is exposed only when avalanches slip in massive sheets from its flanks. At other times of the year the barren slabs are like huge, near-vertical parking lots. After rains or during spring melting, waterfalls cascade down the face, and in fall the foreground colours provide additional appeal. This is the most striking feature visible from the Coquihalla Highway. There are rest areas on both sides of the road with good views of the ridge above. There are pleasant picnic spots, and a hiking trail to Zoa Peak on the ridge is a good day trip for even better views.

From Hope take Highway 5, forty kilometres north to the Zopkios Rest Area, now part of Coquihalla River Provincial Recreation Area.

Hiking routes from nearby Falls Lake can be reached by a turnoff just east of the rest area. Caution should be exercised to ensure hikers don't get onto terrain too exposed for their abilities.

ADAMS RIVER SOCKEYE RUN

• **Feature:** World's largest sockeye salmon run • **Usual Access:** Roadside and easy walks • **Time Required:** Half day from Chase • **Nearest Highway:** Highway 1 (Trans-Canada) • **Best Time To Visit:** October • **Maps:** NTS 1:50,000 82L/13; Outdoor Recreation Council - #7 Shuswap Lake Region 1:100,000

THE ADAMS RIVER is not significant in length or water volume like many great rivers of British Columbia. From its headwaters at the outlet of Adams Lake it runs just eleven kilometres before emptying into Shuswap Lake. However, it is the scene of an internationally significant natural event — the spawning of the sockeye.

Every four years, in mid-October, millions of sockeye salmon return to the Adams River, a tributary of the Fraser, to complete their life cycle. After the eggs are laid in the clean gravels of the streambed, the parents die. Many of the eggs do not survive the winter. Birds such as dippers and gulls feed voraciously on them in fall and early winter. Those surviving the winter hatch in the spring. The fry make their way downstream to Shuswap Lake where they spend their first year before heading for the open sea. Three years later they battle upstream for nearly five hundred kilometres in less than three weeks to repeat the process. More than two million return some years.

This memorable natural event takes place in Roderick Haig-Brown Provincial Park, near the town of Chase on the Trans-Canada Highway. Thousands of people make the journey every year to view the spectacle, significant even in non-peak years.

To view the spawning, take the Trans-Canada Highway eleven kilometres north from Chase to Squilax. Leaving the highway, follow the signs north, crossing the Adams River, then proceeding to the parking lot, a distance of 3.8 kilometres from the Trans-Canada.

Exhibits, pleasant riverside trails to viewing platforms, and park interpreters who give talks and guided walks provide a variety of ways to learn about the spawn.

The spawning salmon support a rich wildlife population. Both the newly-laid eggs and the carcasses of adult salmon provide sustenance for black bears, otters, mink, eagles, and fish-eating waterfowl. Hiking the eighteen kilometres of trails winding through the forest and along both banks of the Adams River will increase the chances of seeing wildlife. While hiking be aware of poison ivy in the area. There's a campground nearby at Shuswap Lake Provincial Park.

CACHE CREEK GRASSLANDS

• **Feature:** Rolling grasslands • **Usual Access:** Roadside • **Time Required:** Three-hour driving loop from Cache Creek • **Nearest Highway:** Highway 1 (Trans-Canada) • **Best Time To Visit:** May to October • **Maps:** BC Forest Service Recreation Sites - Lillooet Area

THE DRY GRASSLANDS around Cache Creek are grazing country for cattle, but are also a special natural feature of British Columbia. The terrain is gently rolling with clumps of trees limited to moister areas and higher elevations. Small lakes, many rimmed with whitish alkaline salts, dot the landscape. Interesting species of mammals, birds, and flowering plants especially suited to life in this hot, dry region can be seen. Places with little or no grazing are rare here. There are plans to establish a provincial park representing the natural feature of grasslands.

A good way to experience typical grassland terrain here is a circular driving tour, beginning and ending at Cache Creek. Take Highway 97 eleven kilometres north from Cache Creek, turning west onto the Lillooet Road (Highway 12). The route leads past small ranches and open forests of Douglas fir and ponderosa pine, especially scenic in spring when wildflowers are at their best.

The Hat Creek Road branches south (left) off the Lillooet Road through rolling grassland, past small lakes, and through shimmering aspen groves, especially beautiful in the fall when they turn golden yellow. At the 19.5-kilometre mark turn left up Oregon Jack Creek. The road climbs over a ridge and is slippery when wet, and narrow in places. About ten kilometres up, a rough road accesses Cornwall Lookout for a good overview of the area. Return to the Oregon Jack Road and continue to the Trans-Canada. Turn left and travel eighteen kilometres to Cache Creek. This circuit takes about three hours.

SPAHATS CREEK FALLS

• **Feature:** Deep gorge and waterfall • **Usual Access:** Short walk from roadside • **Time Required:** One hour from Clearwater • **Nearest Highway:** Highway 5 • **Best Time To Visit:** May to October • **Maps:** NTS 1:50,000 82M/13; BC Parks brochure - Wells Gray Park

THIS WATERFALL in Spahats Creek Provincial Park is

over sixty metres high but is often overlooked by visitors intent on seeing the famous Helmcken Falls in Wells Gray Park, a few kilometres down the Clearwater Valley Road. Spahats Falls have a special appeal: their slender cascade appears to come out of a cave in the rock as Spahats Creek plunges out of a narrow gorge and falls sixty-one metres. It then flows another five hundred metres to join the Clearwater River. There's an excellent access trail, a well placed viewing platform, and interesting exhibits describing the geology of the area. The ten-minute trails to the viewpoint are easy for most visitors.

From the community of Clearwater take Clearwater Valley Road west towards Wells Gray Park for ten kilometres to a parking lot. From here it's a four-hundred-metre walk to the viewpoint.

The twenty-five-site campground in Spahats Creek Provincial park makes a good home base for exploring other features of the area.

TROPHY MOUNTAINS

• **Feature:** Mountain meadows • **Usual Access:** Day hike • **Time Required:** Full day from Clearwater • **Nearest Highway:** Highway 5 • **Best Time To Visit:** July to August • **Maps:** NTS 1:50,000 82M/13; BC Parks brochure - Wells Gray Park

THE TROPHY MOUNTAINS are a range of high, rolling summits, with rounded tops and beautiful subalpine meadows, just outside the eastern boundary of Wells Gray Provincial Park. Many varieties of alpine flowers are found in the extensive meadows, reached by a fairly arduous hike, usually done as an overnight backpacking trip. Indian paintbrush of the palest pinks and yellows, and vast expanses of lupine among scattered clumps of stunted fir are just some

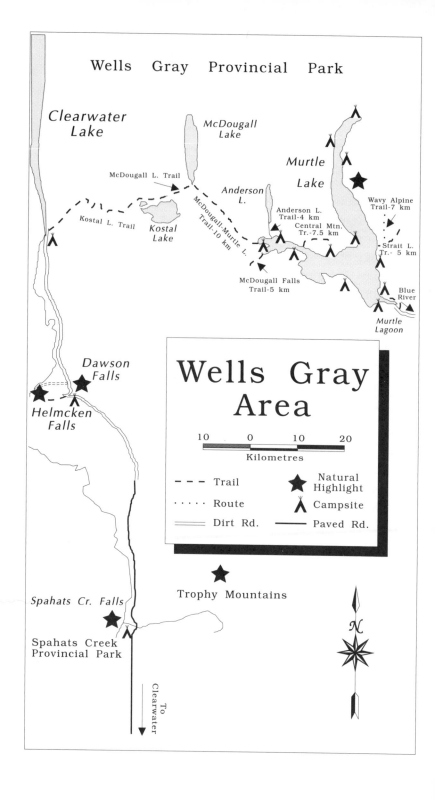

of the floral highlights here in mid-summer. The intensity of the bloom varies from year to year depending on the previous year's weather conditions, but it is always, at the very least, tremendous.

Take Highway 5 to Clearwater then turn west on Clearwater Road and follow signs for Wells Gray Park. After 11.5 kilometres turn east for four kilometres to the turnoff for the Trophy Mountains Trail. Continue fifteen kilometres to the trail head. It is a one-to-two-hour hike up to the best meadows, but time seems to go by quickly once there, especially if you hike with photographers. Allow a full day so the most energetic can hike to the high ridges and others can intensively explore the meadows below.

DAWSON FALLS

• **Feature:** Waterfall • **Usual Access:** Two-to-three-minute walk from roadside • **Time Required:** Half day from Clearwater • **Nearest Highway:** Highway 5 • **Best Time To Visit:** May to October • **Maps:** NTS 1:50,000 82M/13; BC Parks brochure - Wells Gray Park

DAWSON FALLS are among seven major waterfalls in Wells Gray Park. An hour's drive north of the town of Clearwater, the Wells Gray area is world-famous for outstanding natural features, five of which are included in this book. Dawson Falls has a special character. It is one of the few major waterfalls that a visitor can experience from within. It is possible, during some water conditions, to take a walk behind the thundering curtain of the Murtle River as nine thousand cubic metres of water per second plummet twenty metres over a vertical drop.

Many visitors, especially those from eastern Canada, remark that this cascade resembles a down-sized Niagara Falls. Like Niagara, these falls do not require heroic effort to

Dawson Falls in Wells Gray Park.

experience. They are situated at the roadside within a minute or two of the parking lot. As a first stop in the park they are a tantalizing advertisement for other natural delights nearby.

From Clearwater on Highway 5 take Clearwater Valley Road west for forty-one kilometres. At the parking lot for the falls walk one or two minutes to the viewpoint at the brink of the falls. For the more energetic there are trails to the river below the falls. These require caution as rocks are slippery here and the torrent swift.

In spring, wild roses, arnicas, and lupines bloom near the falls in the forest. These are a tiny sample of the 650 upland species found in the park. Fall brings a large variety of mushrooms and striking displays of aspens, slashes of gold against the rich green of the conifers.

Dawson Falls Campground is five hundred metres beyond the falls parking lot. It's a popular base from which to explore other attractions such as Helmcken Falls, the Mushbowl, Clearwater Lake, Murtle River Trail, Stillwater Trail, and the civilized facilities of the town of Clearwater. There are only ten sites, so arrive early in the day during summer to ensure a spot. More camping is available at Clearwater Lake Campground farther along the park road.

HELMCKEN FALLS

• **Feature:** Waterfall • **Usual Access:** One-minute walk from roadside • **Time Required:** Half day from Clearwater • **Nearest Highway:** Highway 5 • **Best Time To Visit:** Year round • **Maps:** NTS 1:50,000 82M/13; BC Parks brochure - Wells Gray Park

HELMCKEN FALLS are the most outstanding of the many waterfalls in Wells Gray Park, considered by many to be among the most impressive falls in Canada. For several years they have graced the cover of telephone books in British Columbia. These falls, on the Murtle River, shoot over 137 metres into a spray-carved amphitheatre, easily viewed from a platform near the parking lot, or from other angles requiring more effort to reach.

The free-falling river volume displaces air near the base, firing jets of wind outward and upward. Because this is the interior wet belt of the province, misty mornings are common, with low cloud or fog obscuring the brink of the falls, giving the impression that it comes directly from the heavens. In winter, during extreme cold snaps, a volcano-shaped ice cone sometimes forms at the base of the falls, building to as much as fifty metres. Every day seems to bring a different look, always inspiring superlatives from visitors.

From Clearwater on Highway 5, take Clearwater Valley Road west for forty-two kilometres to the turnoff to Helmcken Falls. Go a few hundred metres to the parking lot.

There are several vantage points, each requiring a different amount of effort, from a short walk to a strenuous knee-burning day hike. The usual access is to walk a few metres

Helmcken Falls in Wells Gray Park.

from the Helmcken Falls parking lot to a platform lookout. This gives an unobstructed view of the falls and the massive cavern that has been carved out of the lava bed.

For another interesting angle hike a four-kilometre trail to the cliffs near the brink of the falls. It's an easy hike along the Murtle River from the Mushbowl area, but take care near the falls as the spray makes rocks slippery: it's a one-way trip if you slip over the edge.

A good but difficult view is from near the base of the falls. The trail leads from the viewing platform along the rim of the gorge, then down to the river. It takes two to four hours of hard effort to reach the halfway point on this hike. The hardest part, after viewing the falls, is retracing your steps four hours uphill. This trip is not for the fainthearted.

When a government surveyor discovered the falls in 1913 he wanted to name them for the premier, Richard McBride. The B.C. premier, in turn, suggested they be named after Dr. John S. Helmcken, a former speaker of the legislature. Unfortunately, Helmcken died without seeing the wonderful natural feature named for him.

This waterfall is the highlight of the area for most people. However, there is so much to see in this 529,748-hectare park that several days should be allowed for a good visit.

There are campsites at Dawson Falls, at Clearwater Lake farther along the Clearwater Valley Road, and at Spahats Creek Provincial Park nearby.

MURTLE LAKE

• **Feature:** Large scenic lake • **Usual Access:** One to one-and-a-half-hour portage • **Time Required:** Two to ten days • **Nearest Highway:** Highway 5 • **Best Time To Visit:** July to October • **Maps:** NTS 1:50,000 83D/04; BC Parks brochure - Wells Gray Park

EXTRAORDINARILY PICTURESQUE, Murtle Lake is the largest in Wells Gray Provincial Park. Though at a total of 76.3 square kilometres it ranks only 33d among the province's largest lakes, it is, at 333 metres, the 6th deepest. It's a canoeists' haven, with fourteen campsites around the shores, and hiking trails leading from the lake to the surrounding wilderness. Non-paddlers can take a portage trail to the lake, about an hour and a half return.

From Blue River on Highway 5, travel the four-wheel-drive road twenty-six kilometres to Murtle Lake trail head. Canoes must be portaged 2.5 kilometres to Murtle Lake.

To maintain the pristine nature, hunting, power boats, and off-road motorized vehicles are banned. There is often excellent fishing for Dolly Varden char here and chances of seeing wildlife, such as black bears and mule deer, are also good. This peacefulness is what originally prompted its name when it reminded a C.P.R. surveyor of his Scottish birthplace.

It takes five to seven days to paddle the shoreline of Murtle Lake, with endless variations possible by shortcutting either of the two long arms. Winds can whip up the water at times. It is best to keep near shore unless conditions are good, always watching the weather, which can change quickly in the mountains.

Several trails begin from the shores of Murtle Lake. Hikes may be taken to Anderson Lake, Strait Lake, McDougall Falls, and the stunning views from Central Mountain Trail. All day trips and trail heads are located close to camping areas. There are fourteen wilderness campsites on the lake including one with a sleeping shelter.

A challenging forty-four-kilometre backpacking trip can be done from Murtle Lake to Clearwater Lake. Backpackers must first canoe to the McDougall Lake trail head on the west side of Murtle Lake. From here hike past McDougall and Kostal lakes to the trail's end at Clearwater Lake Road. Backpackers can be picked up here by vehicle, or return along the same route back to Murtle Lake.

The BC Parks brochure, available from the visitors' centre, has a good map showing trails and camps.

Services and accommodation are available in Blue River.

REARGUARD FALLS

• **Feature:** Salmon leaping up falls • **Usual Access:** Roadside • **Time Required:** One hour from Mount Robson • **Nearest Highway:** Highway 5 • **Best Time To Visit:** Late July to mid August • **Maps:** NTS 1:50,000 82M/13

REARGUARD FALLS is the final obstacle for the thousands of salmon returning up the Fraser River system to spawn. A steep cascade in the emerald green river, it proves just formidable enough to prevent the fish from progressing any further. The falls are the main feature of Rearguard Falls Provincial Park, just west of Mount Robson on the Yellowhead Highway.

The well-trodden trails take only a few minutes to reach fenced viewing areas on cliffs above the falls. The salmon can be seen in mid to late August, leaping in vain against the powerful cascade. Through sheer determination some almost make it. At times crowds of onlookers spontaneously cheer them onward but few fish have been known to breach Rearguard Falls.

Coming west from Mount Robson, the parking lot is ten kilometres west of the park boundary. From Tete Jaune Cache junction travel east for four kilometres on Highway 16 to a parking lot on the south side of the highway. There are trails, about fifteen minutes return, down to viewpoints overlooking the falls. There are some views from the parking lot but the best are from the lower viewpoints. Over the years more adventurous types have made other trails leading to the brink of the falls. Exercise extreme caution if you find yourself near the water as the rocks are slick.

There are campgrounds nearby in Mount Robson Provincial Park and in Valemount, twenty-nine kilometres west via Highways 16 and 5.

VALLEY OF A THOUSAND FALLS

• **Feature:** Major waterfalls • **Usual Access:** Backpack
• **Nearest Highway:** Highway 16 • **Time Required:** Overnight from Jasper or Valemount • **Best Time To Visit:** July to September • **Maps:** NTS 1:50,000 83D/15; BC Parks brochure - Mt. Robson

THE VALLEY of a Thousand Falls, on the west side of Mount Robson, features Canada's highest concentration of major waterfalls. It is flanked by Mount Robson and Mount Whitehorn, in Mount Robson Provincial Park. White Falls, Falls of the Pool, and Emperor Falls are the most magnificant. All three are on the Robson River adjacent to a four-kilometre stretch of hiking trail. Several good campsites are

Valley of a Thousand Falls in Mount Robson Park.

well situated to make the most of the valley's scenery. As the name suggests, it sometimes seems as if there are a thousand falls pouring into the valley. After a downpour, the cliff-sides weep with hundreds of nameless lacy cascades. High above, the robin's-egg hues of a dozen glaciers overhang the valley, occasionally sending large blocks of ice thundering down. Everywhere is the sound of rushing waters. This is the most popular backpacking trail in the Rockies.

The Valley of a Thousand Falls may be visited as an overnight backpacking trip on the Berg Lake Trail. It begins at the Mount Robson Information Centre, eighty-four kilometres west of Jasper, Alberta, and 16.5 kilometres east of Tete Jaune Cache on Highway 16. Campground fees for sites along the Berg Lake Trail must be paid here before setting out. Park brochures with good trail maps, current trail conditions, bear activity reports, and other useful information are also available here.

The Berg Lake Trail parking lot is at the end of a two-kilometre road heading north from the information centre. Cross a footbridge at the north end of the trail-head parking lot, then take the Berg Lake Trail along the west side of the Robson River for 4.5 kilometres to Kinney Lake. The trail crosses to the east side of the river on a footbridge at the south end of the lake. Continue on to the north end of the lake to Kinney Lake Campground at kilometre 7.2. There are twelve sites, a cooking shelter, food hanging platforms, and firewood.

Beyond Kinney Lake, the trail enters the Valley of a Thousand Falls. At kilometre ten is Whitehorn Camp, scenically situated beside the turquoise rush of the Robson River, with Mount Whitehorn commanding the view up the valley. Here too, is a cooking shelter, food-hanging apparatus, and firewood. This is the last camp before the beginning of a steep climb to Emperor Falls. Those not intending to overnight beyond the Valley of a Thousand Falls should camp here, or at Kinney Lake, to eliminate lugging a heavy pack five

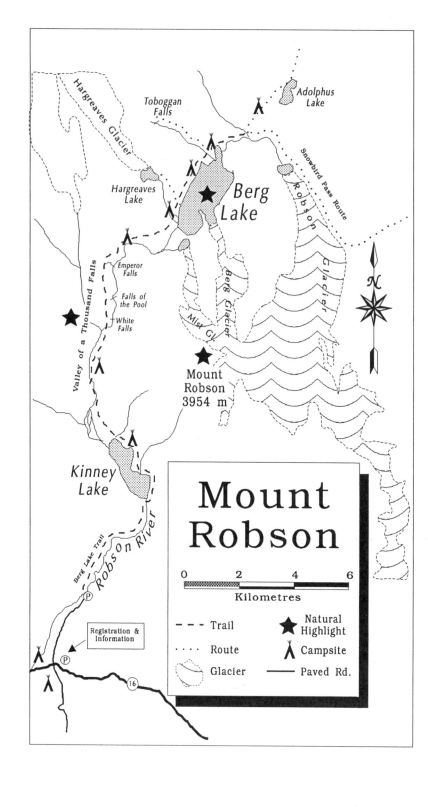

kilometres up to the next camping area, above Emperor Falls.

The section of trail beyond Whitehorn Campground offers continuous awesome sights. Soon after leaving Whitehorn Campground the steep climb begins alongside the gorge of the swiftest section of the Robson River. Beginning in Berg Lake, on Mount Robson's north side, the Robson River flows west. It detours around the giant mountain mass before turning south and entering the Valley of a Thousand Falls. Confined to a narrow gorge, it descends more than eight hundred metres in 1.6 kilometres. The trail is never far from this dynamic section of the river, which contains the mightiest falls in the park.

White Falls, at kilometre 11.8, is the first of the major falls encountered during the ascent. It is followed by Falls of the Pool, at kilometre 12.7, and Emperor Falls, at kilometre 16.

Emperor Falls is the highlight of the valley. Just a few metres below the brink the water strikes a huge rock step. This launches the cascade outward with great force, producing a horsetail form that has become one of the trademark sights of the park.

Beyond Emperor Falls, after one short steep section, the trail levels out, and it's an easy five kilometres to Berg Lake, one of the most picturesque areas of the Rockies. See this book's description of Berg Glacier for information about this area.

BERG GLACIER

• **Feature:** Advancing glacier • **Usual Access:** Backpack or helicopter • **Time Required:** One to two days from Jasper or Valemount • **Nearest Highway:** Highway 5 • **Best Time To Visit:** June to September • **Maps:** NTS 1:50,000 83D/15; BC Parks brochure - Mt. Robson

MOUNT ROBSON Provincial Park abuts the western

Mount Robson, highest peak in the Canadian Rockies.

boundary of Jasper National Park and features one of the few advancing glaciers in the province. The eight-hundred-metre width of Berg Glacier tumbles over a kilometre and a half down the north side of Mount Robson and bears a suitable alternate name — Tumbling Glacier. Huge turquoise blocks of ice crash directly into Berg Lake from the glacier's snout. The seemingly immobile glacier emits thunderous grunts and groans as it slowly creeps down the mountain to the lake. Only those willing to make the backpacking journey (or prosperous enough to take the chopper) to the north side of the Rockies' highest peak get to see this fine natural feature. It is not visible from the highway viewpoint on the south side.

Known affectionately as the backside of Robson, the area may be reached via the most popular trail in the Rockies, the Berg Lake Trail. Requiring at least one overnight on the trail, campers must first register and pay camping fees at the Mount Robson Information Centre. It is located on Highway 16, 2.5 kilometres east of the western park boundary or fifty-nine kilometres west of the eastern entrance at Yellowhead Pass. An access road travels two kilometres north to the Berg Lake trail head and parking lot at the Robson River.

Reaching Berg Glacier from the trail head requires a strong heart, lungs, and legs as it has some steep sections. Follow the same directions as for Valley of a Thousand Falls, continuing beyond Emperor Falls another five kilometres to Berg Lake.

Marmot Campground is the first within sight of Berg Glacier but there are only six pads for tents. Two kilometres farther, at Berg Lake Campground, there are twenty pads. Fairly civilized as backcountry campgrounds go, it has a cooking shelter and barbecues. The views of the glacier and the mountain face are far better than at Marmot Campground, although, some people prefer the smaller number of neighbours at Marmot Campground. Berg Lake Campground is twenty-one kilometres from the trail head, a long haul for one day, but worth the effort to spend more time in the lake area. This campsite is a good base for exploring the area. It is convenient to the trails giving the best views of the Berg Glacier. Scores of other scenic delights, most of which are within sight of Berg Glacier, can be seen in the area, warranting a multiday stay. Wildflowers such as yellow dryas and willow herb decorate the gravel flats adjacent to the lake.

An excellent network of day-hike-length trails provides varied views of the north side of Mount Robson and the Tumbling Glacier. Routes to Toboggan Falls, Hargreaves Lake, Mumm Peak, Snowbird Pass, and Robson Glacier, all offer tremendous views of the massive north side of Mount Robson.

An interesting alternative to hiking back out the Berg Lake Trail is to continue past Berg Lake via Adolphus Lake and the Moose River to the Yellowhead Highway near Moose Lake. This makes a challenging seven-to-ten-day hike for experienced backcountry travellers.

MOUNT ROBSON

• **Feature:** Highest summit in Canadian Rockies • **Usual Access:** Roadside • **Time Required:** Two hours from Jasper • **Nearest Highway:** Highway 5 • **Best Time To Visit:** Year round • **Maps:** NTS 1:50,000 83D/15; BC Parks brochure - Mt. Robson

MOUNT ROBSON, at 3,954 metres, is the highest peak in the Canadian Rockies. It stands guard over the valley of the Robson River and is the highlight of the drive on the Yellowhead (Highway 16) between Jasper, Alberta, and Valemount, B.C., in east central B.C. It is, naturally, the dominant feature of Mount Robson Provincial Park.

Although conveniently situated beside the highway, it's often obscured by clouds. Because it is so massive, it makes its own weather: clouds often conceal the summit while surrounding peaks are clear. The visitor who happens to be in the area on a perfectly clear day is lucky. Using high-powered binoculars or a spotting scope, climbers can be seen on the south-side route to the summit. It is a challenge not to be overlooked by any serious Rocky mountaineer, and one of the most memorable sights for motorists along the Yellowhead Highway.

Take Yellowhead Highway to the Mount Robson Information Centre, sixteen kilometres east of Tete Jaune Cache junction, or fifty-nine kilometres west of Jasper National Park boundary. For most visitors it is satisfying enough to look from the highway at the south side of the mountain. From

Mount Robson seen from the Yellowhead Highway.

the parking lot at the Mount Robson Information Centre it isn't even necessary to get out of the car for a great view. For those approaching from the west, the mountain commands the view from the entrance of the park to the Information Centre, a distance of 2.5 kilometres.

Some travellers are tempted to climb to the summit. Mount Robson is a classic of North American mountaineering, attracting climbers from all over the world. There is no easy scramble route to the top. All routes are long and dangerous: experience in climbing high, difficult peaks is a prerequisite.

Credit for first reaching the summit goes to Colonel W.W. Foster, A.H. McCarthy, and the alpine guide Conrad Kain who climbed it in 1913. It had already been referred to as Mount Robson for seventy years by the time of the first ascent, but it is still uncertain for whom it was named. Some theories suggest it was John Robson, the premier of B.C. from 1889 to 1892. Others think the name refers to Colin Robertson who, in 1820, sent a party of natives on a fur-seeking expedition in the area.

Mount Robson Provincial Park, a total of 219,829 hectares, has over two hundred kilometres of trails, numerous glaciers, waterfalls, white-water rivers, and turquoise lakes set amid the high peaks of the continental divide. Good camping is available in the park and other accommodation can be found within an hour's drive, either at Valemount to the west, or Jasper National Park to the east.

BOTANIE VALLEY WILDFLOWERS

• **Feature:** Aridland wildflowers • **Usual Access:** Rough gravel road • **Time Required:** Two hours from Lytton • **Nearest Highway:** Highway 12 • **Best Time To Visit:** Late May to late June • **Maps:** BC Forest Service Recreation Sites - Lillooet Area

BOTANIE MOUNTAIN separates the Thompson and the Fraser, just before the two great rivers meet at Lytton. In spring, it comes alive with wildflowers, outshining higher, steeper summits still cloaked in snow. In the Thompson Indian language Botanie means "covered," apparently a reference to mist that sometimes covers the area. The name also conveniently describes the attraction the area has for visitors from all over the globe. They come here for botany, to witness the profusion of aridland wildflowers that beautify the landscape in spring and early summer. Also attractive is its convenient location, accessible to motorists, a short drive from the Trans-Canada Highway town of Lytton.

A half-hour drive from Lytton takes you to the major blossom area around Botanie Lake. From Lytton take Highway 12 north, cross the Thompson River bridge, continue four hundred metres, then turn east on the Botanie Creek Road. The road rises steadily, soon skirting a gorge with a massive grey rock face, its barrenness made appealing by an intricate network of whitish veins. Continuing up Botanie Valley, the road travels through open stands of ponderosa pine and interior Douglas fir, splashes of wildflower clumps brightening the forest floor. Arrow leaf balsamroot is a dramatic and early bloomer, its large, sunflower-like blossoms announcing spring in mid to late April. Travel later in May and early June to see the area during the peak display.

Wildflower enthusiasts usually congregate around Botanie Lake at kilometre 16.7 to photograph, study, or simply smell the flowers. Bear in mind that the lake is on Indian land which should be respected. There are no power boats allowed on the lake. If you pick the flowers, they will die in a few hours, whereas leaving them will enrich the next visitor's experience.

A B.C. Forest Service campsite just before the lake is available free for primitive overnight camping and is accessible to cars and motorhomes.

For ambitious types, there is a hiking route to the top of

Botanie Ridge via an old Forest Service lookout road. Along the way are good views of the Lytton area. From the top there's a panoramic view of the Fraser-Thompson confluence.

To get to the trail head for the hike turn west at the 6.8-kilometre point of the Botanie Creek Road onto a rough dirt road. It continues for about five hundred metres to the beginning of the hike. The trail follows the switchbacking old road up to the left. A shortcut just after the sign for Moose Flats is the more direct approach to the ridgetop where it is about three kilometres to the lookout. The Stein Valley is to the west, thickly forested for the time being. This is a dry trip and can be extremely hot in summer so take plenty of water, sunscreen, and a good sun hat.

LOWER STEIN VALLEY

• **Feature:** Pristine river valley • **Usual Access:** Day hike or backpack • **Time Required:** One to multiday • **Nearest Highway:** Highway 1 (Trans-Canada) • **Best Time To Visit:** May to October • **Maps:** BC Forest Service Recreation Sites - Lillooet Area

THE STEIN VALLEY has been a special place to the natives of the Lytton area for hundreds, perhaps thousands, of years. It has an overwhelming feeling of peace. Recently non-natives have discovered its economic and spiritual resources, making it one of the major fronts of the B.C. environmental war since the early 1980s. The issue, to log or not to log, is still not settled.

The Stein River is a crystal clear tumbling torrent, flowing east from the rugged mountains east of Lillooet Lake, through the last unlogged watershed within a few hours of Vancouver. It is home to grizzly and black bears, deer, and mountain goats. A wet microclimate allows trees such as giant red cedars to grow here, just a few kilometres from one of the hottest, driest places in Canada.

Hundreds of Indian pictographs add to the spiritual nature of the place. Even the most jaded wilderness travellers acknowledge that the Stein has a special feeling to it. In recent years a trail has been improved to reach the upper end of the valley, and although best visited as a weekend backpacking trip, even a day hike can reveal the specialness of this remarkable place.

Take the Trans-Canada Highway to Lytton and turn onto Highway 12. Travel north, crossing the Thompson River bridge then take the Lytton Ferry Road left. This is a free ferry, powered primarily by the force of the Fraser River's current, working on a system of cables, pulleys, and rudders. It takes two vehicles per trip and usually there is a wait of only a few minutes. There are times during spring runoff when it does not operate.

After leaving the ferry, travel north on the gravel road for about five kilometres until you see a large homemade sign on a tree on the left, indicating the Stein Heritage Trail. Take a very rough road to the left for a few hundred metres to the trail-head parking lot where there is a much more substantial sign between two rock cairns. The lower Stein Valley is visible from here.

The lower Stein may be explored on a day trip, the length of which will depend on the abilities of the hiker. Even a couple of hours' return trip is well worth it. A good full day would take you to a cable crossing and back, a distance of twenty kilometres requiring eight to ten hours.

The trail follows the river from the dry terrain of the trail head into cool, dark forests of Douglas fir and even cedars. There are numerous camping areas that serve as good rest stops, usually near the river, handy for refilling canteens. Along the way are many pictographs, or Indian rock art.

Relics of old cabins remain. Three hours from the trail head is Tepee Camp, the most popular campsite in the valley, in a small clearing overlooking the river. There is the frame of a tepee here, handy for hanging food to discourage bears.

This valley has been a home to Indians for generations: newcomers should treat it, as natives do, with respect. Smoke from campfires and oil from your fingers can damage pictographs: they should be admired but not touched, and campfires should be some distance away. There is no need to establish new campsites or fire pits when several already exist. Fire here is a serious hazard during the tinder-dry weather in summer.

There are healthy bear populations in the valley, both black and grizzly, so make enough noise on the trail to avoid surprising them, and hang food when camping overnight. There are some campsites with good food-hanging structures already established. Wood ticks inhabit the valley, so ensure you know how to remove these unpleasant pests.

Farwell Canyon on the Chilcotin River.

Cariboo-Chilcotin

The Cariboo-Chilcotin stretches almost the entire width of the province, from the western slope of the Cariboo Mountains in the east to the Pacific Ocean in the west, spanning central B.C. Popular with outdoor recreationists, Cariboo-Chilcotin features the remote waters of fiordlands and archipelagos in the coastal areas on its western fringes. Farther inland, but not far from roads, are major waterfalls, and multi-coloured mountain ranges. Canoeists will find a world famous wilderness canoe expedition in this region, and mountaineers may be drawn to the highest mountain entirely within the province's boundaries — Mount Waddington, rising to 4,016 metres.

Highway 97 from Cache Creek crosses the eastern part of the region, running through Williams Lake and Quesnel on its way to Prince George. Highway 20 connects Williams Lake with the coastal community of Bella Coola, 465 kilometres to the west.

The Fraser River runs south through the eastern half of this region. East of the Fraser River is the Cariboo area, dotted with lakes and evergreen forests. West of the Fraser River is ranching country, rolling grasslands and pockets of pine forest. Farther along is the formidable ragged outline of the Coast Range, including Mount Waddington. West of the Coast Range, the Inside Passage route threads its way through hundreds of islands. The entire region is known as the land of lakes, providing plenty of options for freshwater fishing. Being one of the sunniest, driest parts of the

Cariboo-
Chilcotin

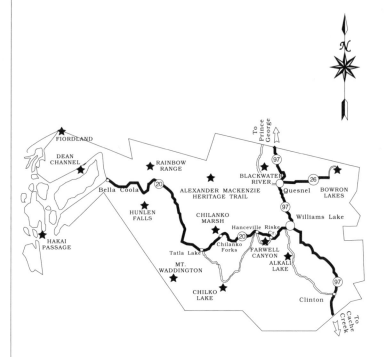

FIORDLAND

DEAN
CHANNEL

RAINBOW
RANGE

BLACKWATER
RIVER

To
Prince
George

97

26

BOWRON
LAKES

Bella Coola

20

ALEXANDER MACKENZIE
HERITAGE TRAIL

Quesnel

HUNLEN
FALLS

CHILANKO
MARSH

97

Williams Lake

HAKAI
PASSAGE

Tatla Lake

Chilanko
Forks

Hanceville Riske
Cr.

20

MT.
WADDINGTON

CHILKO
LAKE

FARWELL
CANYON

ALKALI
LAKE

97

Clinton

To
Cache
Creek

Vancouver

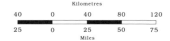

Maintained highway

Forestry road

Natural highlight

Kilometres

| 40 | 0 | 40 | 80 | 120 |

| 25 | 0 | 25 | 50 | 75 |

Miles

province, vacationers planning to visit here have a good chance of having fair weather.

Parks and recreation areas contain many of the natural attractions of this region. In the coastal section is Hakai Recreation Area, a mecca for salmon fishers, ocean kayakers, and boaters. Fiordland Recreation Area also draws paddlers and cruisers to its classic waterways. Freshwater paddlers come from all over to spend a week or so on a wilderness canoe loop in Bowron Lake Provincial Park, while hikers and backpackers are drawn to the Rainbow Range and majestic Hunlen Falls, in Tweedsmuir Provincial Park. This region has exciting adventures for everyone.

While experiencing these natural highlights, visitors should keep a keen eye out for wildlife, which is plentiful. Marine mammals are common sights during the coastal trips. Porpoises and whales are almost sure bets. Land-based trips run through grizzly and black bear country in this region with the added potential of viewing caribou, wolves, moose, deer, goats and thousands of waterfowl during spring and fall migrations.

The climate is extremely diverse in this region, ranging from misty fiords on the west coast, to hot, dry, grasslands in the central rangelands, to cool meadows of the Cariboo Mountains in the east. Light clothing and large doses of insect repellent should see you through most of the lower elevations. If visiting the coast, add good wet-weather gear to your list. Occasional "cold snaps" during spring and fall make warm, layered clothing a must in the mountains.

ALKALI LAKE

• **Feature:** White pelicans • **Usual Access:** Roadside • **Time Required:** Half day from Williams Lake • **Nearest Highway:** Highway 97 • **Best Time To Visit:** May and October

BIRDERS COMING to this tiny lake, in the dry ranch country southwest of Williams Lake, should keep an eye out for white pelicans, an endangered species in British Columbia. They nest in only one location in the province, several kilometres north of Alkali Lake, but access is restricted there during the breeding season because of their sensitivity to disturbance. In May and June they visit Alkali Lake almost daily, feeding mainly on small fish. Once thought to be a threat to freshwater sport fisheries, it is known now that most of the fish caught by the white pelican are non-sport species. B.C.'s entire population of white pelicans amounts to only three hundred individuals. Visitors are fortunate to have an easily accessible spot such as Alkali Lake to view this fascinating and rare resident of the province.

Alkali Lake is an hour's drive from Williams Lake, just right for a half-day outing. There are approaches from the south or north: the fastest is the northern option, from Williams Lake. Take Highway 20 west from Williams Lake for two kilometres to Big Bar Road, then travel south on Big Bar Road for forty-three kilometres. The lake is on the west side of the road, two hundred metres beyond Alkali Lake Ranch.

Reaching Alkali Lake from the south is longer and dustier. Take Highway 97 north from Clinton for ten kilometres, then turn west on Big Bar Road. It's a rough gravel road for 107 kilometres to the lake, just south of the Alkali Lake community.

Watch the sky for a line or V formation of large white birds with black wingtips. They soar high on thermals, alternately flapping their wings and gliding, necks tucked in like herons. The white pelican's wingspan is one of the largest of North American birds, measuring nearly three metres. It is able to ride air currents extremely efficiently on forays as far as two hundred kilometres from its nest. Unlike brown pelicans, white pelicans do not make crashing dives into the water to feed. Instead, they often fish in groups, wading in the shallows. By dipping their heads beneath the surface and extracting five to six litres of water in their bill pouches, then straining it out, they catch small fish, frogs, and salamanders.

If you see a pelican bearing a small blue wing tag, the Ministry of Environment in Williams Lake should be notified. These tags are part of a project to learn more about the birds' migration habits.

Birders enjoy the area around Alkali Lake for more than the pelicans: there are many interesting species here, including mountain bluebirds, western meadowlarks, black terns, kestrels, and ruddy ducks. Be sure to bring binoculars or a spotting scope.

There's camping at Big Bar Lake Provincial Park, seventy-three kilometres south of Alkali Lake. There are also private campgrounds around Williams Lake. Free B.C. Forest Service campsites south of Alkali Lake are located at Brigham Springs, Little Big Bar Lake, and Riley Dam. Check with a Travel Infocentre in Clinton or Williams Lake for directions and road conditions.

Visitors should be aware that gravel roads in this area are often used by giant logging trucks, thundering down steep hills, and appearing unexpectedly around tight bends: drivers should leave the birding to passengers until finding a safe parking area off the road.

CHILKO LAKE

• **Feature:** Lake and mountain scenery • **Usual Access:** Roadside • **Time Required:** Weekend from Williams Lake • **Nearest Highway:** Highway 20 • **Best Time To Visit:** June to October • **Maps:** NTS 1:50,000 92N/01,08; BC Forest Service Recreation Sites - Cariboo

CHILKO LAKE is a long narrow waterway, set tight

against the eastern flank of the glacier-crowned Coast Ranges in the Chilcotin country of southwestern B.C. It offers superb views, looking west from the eastern shoreline, of greenish-blue waters backdropped by jagged peaks rising higher than 3,300 metres above sea level. In fall, the lake reflections are of incomparable beauty, aspens becoming golden splashes against the rich green expanses of evergreen forest. Reached by rough logging roads, a visit here is well worth the dust and potholes encountered along the way. Hiking, fishing, and horseback riding are all excellent around Chilko Lake.

Passenger vehicles can handle the roads but large RVs and trailer rigs may have some trouble, depending on conditions. The Travel Infocentre and B.C. Forest Service office in Williams Lake should have current information. There are two usual approaches to Chilko Lake, both from Highway 20. From Williams Lake travel Highway 20 for 226 kilometres west to Tatla Lake. Turning south onto the gravel Tatlayoko-Chilko Lake Road, follow the signs for Chilko Lake Lodge. It is about an hour's drive to the lake from the main highway, skirting several pretty lakes before arriving at the lodge. Campers should continue past the lodge to the B.C. Forest Service campsite where there is free camping at the north end of Chilko Lake. There is a hiking trail from the campsite up Tullin Mountain giving excellent overviews of the area. There are also Forest Service campsites along the road in at Cochin Lake and Choelquoit Lake. Chilko Lake Lodge has canoe, power boat, and horse rentals, and helicopter tours.

Another road runs through an even more scenic area of Chilko Lake. It is a longer route on dirt, however, and is more variable in its conditions. Check at the Infocentre in Williams Lake before setting out. From Hanceville on Highway 20, ninety kilometres west of Williams Lake, go south on the Chilko Lake Road. It's a two-to-three-hour run to Chilko Lake, but there is excellent camping at a Forest Service campsite at the lake or at several other sites along the road from Hanceville. Be sure to get a forestry map and current information before taking this route: roads here are often not well signed and can be confusing.

CHILANKO MARSH

- **Feature:** Wetlands wildlife • **Usual Access:** Roadside
- **Time Required:** Overnight (for morning birding)
- **Nearest Highway:** Highway 20 • **Best Time To Visit:** May and October • **Maps:** B.C. Forest Service - Cariboo Region

CHILANKO MARSH is north of Highway 20, near Puntzi Lake, about three hours west of Williams Lake. This rich wetland is home to a wide range of birds, from waterfowl to grassland species. Canada geese, shovelers, and pintails nest here at one of the best birding areas in the Cariboo-Chilcotin. Black terns, yellow-headed blackbirds, and mountain bluebirds are commonly seen.

To get to the marsh take Highway 20 for two hundred kilometres west from Williams Lake to the Puntzi Lake Road. Go north to Puntzi Lake. The marsh is across the road from the airstrip.

Ideally, for birdwatching, the marsh should be visited at dawn in spring, when the birds are most active. You can stay at a private campground at Puntzi Lake for an early start: a few campgrounds are just minutes from the marsh. Also at the lake is a little used B.C. Forest Service campsite. Bull Canyon Provincial Park is sixty kilometres east of the marsh.

RAINBOW RANGE

- **Feature:** Multihued volcanic mountains • **Usual Access:** Backpack • **Time Required:** Two to three days from Williams Lake • **Nearest Highway:** Highway 20 • **Best Time**

Rainbow Range in Tweedsmuir Park.

To Visit: Early July to late September • **Maps:** NTS 1:50,000 93C/12 ,13; BC Parks brochure - Tweedsmuir (South)

THE RAINBOW RANGE is a chain of gentle volcanic summits in the southern portion of Tweedsmuir, B.C.'s largest provincial park. They are appropriately named. Loose volcanic gravels have, over time, been spectacularly streaked red, yellow, and magenta by weathering. Known by Indians as the "Bleeding Mountains," the long red streaks do appear as though the mountains are bleeding. The Rainbows, mostly above treeline, have unlimited hiking routes from open ridge to open ridge. The scores of alpine lakes provide scenic campsites, many near impressive wildflower meadows. Services are not available, so as with all areas in the Tweedsmuir backcountry, visitors should be well equipped and experienced in wilderness travel.

The most direct route to the Rainbow Range is via the "Trail to the Rainbows." From Williams Lake travel Highway 20 west for 360 kilometres to Heckman Pass. Take a signed turnoff road one kilometre north to the parking lot for Octopus Lake. Here the trail to the Rainbow Range starts.

The trail begins across a footbridge and heads directly uphill to the north. Don't take the left trail which goes to Octopus Lake. The steep grade soon becomes more gentle, a gradual ascent leading through meadows, past tiny lakes, and opening up more as you make progress. After two to three hours of hiking past several small lakes and ponds, you reach a lake with a small island near its eastern end. This is locally known as Marmot Lake, scenically situated on a broad plateau of rock gardens, flower meadows, and clusters of gnarled firs. Scores of smaller lakes dot the landscape, highlighted by exceptional views. Far beyond the plateau, in the south and west, are the formidable glacier-laden Coast Mountains. Mount Waddington, at 4,016 metres, the highest peak entirely within B.C., dominates the skyline. There is good camping at the east end of Marmot Lake, but hikers are free to camp anywhere as there are no designated sites.

Another hour beyond Marmot Lake, is a better campsite for views of the red streaks of the Rainbow Range. To reach it, continue northeast from Marmot Lake, keeping high enough on the east slopes of the Tusulko River valley to avoid brush and bogs. There are a few cairns marking the route but they're easily missed: concentrate on the route, using a topographic map, and head for the obvious pass visible at the headwaters of the Tusulko. Stay within sight of the river on the west side and you'll get to the pass in about an hour. Hiking ten minutes more brings you to the more northerly of two small lakes in the pass. An excellent campsite is on the rise north of the lake. Here the Rainbow Range can be seen to the north, while the volcanic formation called the Molar is reflected in the lake to the south. It is twelve kilometres from the beginning of the trail to this campsite, lying at just over eighteen hundred metres above sea level.

There's a pleasant two-hour return walk onto a ridge north

of camp with views of the Beef Trail River and Rainbow Range. They're especially good at sunset when the late light intensifies the colours of the rocks. From the summit of this ridge, scan the hanging valleys of the next range to the east for caribou.

Several day hiking routes on long tundra ridges may be done from this base camp. An excellent full-day hike over five or six low summits may be done from the ridge to the northwest of camp. The connecting ridges are dry so water should be carried. When mist and low clouds obscure the routes in this treeless area it is easy to become disoriented — everything looks the same. Take appropriate maps and be sure someone in the party can read them.

Chances of seeing game, especially caribou, are excellent. They are often spotted on snow patches seeking relief from insects. Grizzly bears and wolves also inhabit these hills but are seen less frequently. To avoid unpleasant night visits, store food away from camp, under rocks if possible.

The most common wildlife, is biting insects. Mosquitos greet hikers in the early morning; horseflies take over during the heat of day, followed closely by blackflies. These pests tend to disappear when the cool alpine night sets in, making way for no-see-ums that invade the tent at every opening. Bring the bug dope. Headnets are useful for this trip and even the hardiest outdoors people have given in, and used them here. September might be a better time to come here if you just can't stand bugs, although the flowers will be finished blooming. Tundra foliage changing colour, however, can be equally appealing.

This area is mainly above the treeline so wood is scarce. Carry a backpacking stove.

HUNLEN FALLS

- **Feature:** Second-highest waterfall in the province • **Usual**

Access: Backpack overnight • **Time Required:** Two days from trail head • **Nearest Highway:** Highway 20 • **Best Time To Visit:** June to September • **Maps:** NTS 1:50,000 93C/05; BC Parks brochure - Tweedsmuir (South)

THE SECOND-HIGHEST waterfall in British Columbia is located in the southern portion of Tweedsmuir Provincial Park, between Williams Lake and Bella Coola. Hunlen Creek flows over a sheer 259 metre drop, forming one of the best known, but lightly visited, features of the park. The drop is dramatic, the way a great waterfall should be. A large gorge has formed at the bottom of the falls, testimony to the erosional forces of falling water during times of peak flow.

To see the falls, take Highway 20 west from Williams Lake for 379 kilometres to the trail head at Young Creek picnic site, in Tweedsmuir Park. The first thirteen kilometres of the twenty-nine kilometre route, along the Atnarko Tote Road, is driveable with a four-wheel-drive vehicle (and some high-clearance two-wheel-drives). If hiking the entire route in, bear in mind that there is no water available along the trail beyond the Stillwater River, so fill up and ration accordingly.

At the end of the Atnarko Tote Road, the hiking trail begins at a parking lot near the Atnarko River. Hike to the footbridge across the Atnarko River. The trail climbs steeply up seventy-eight calf-burning switchbacks, before levelling out for the final five to six kilometres to a campsite at the south end of Turner Lake. From here it is about a half-hour walk along a trail to the falls. Be extremely careful near the edge of the viewpoint.

Once you reach the falls and Turner Lake, it is worth staying a few days to explore. A beautiful alpine area around Ptarmigan Lake is reached via a twelve-kilometre trail from the campsite at Turner Lake. Halfway along the west side of the lake, Turner Lakes Wilderness Camp rents canoes for trips on the lake chain south of the falls.

A note of caution: grizzly bears feed on salmon spawning

in the Atnarko River in the fall and several are resident in the valley year-round. They are extremely dangerous if surprised or threatened. Practise good bear sense, making lots of noise while hiking so you don't surprise them, and don't hike alone here, especially during twilight hours.

This is a wilderness area requiring proper equipment and experience. Check at park headquarters for bear news, and other information before setting out into the back country.

DEAN CHANNEL

• **Feature:** Longest fiord in B.C. • **Usual Access:** Boat or float plane • **Time Required:** Full day from Bella Coola • **Nearest Highway:** Highway 20 • **Best Time To Visit:** June to September

DEAN CHANNEL, midway along the B.C. coast a few kilometres north of Bella Coola, is significant both physically and historically. Physically, it is the longest fiord in the province, more than 120 kilometres. Historically, it was the end of the first overland continental crossing, completed by explorer Alexander Mackenzie in 1793. Unknown to Mackenzie, it had been named Dean Channel just three weeks earlier by Captain George Vancouver, who surveyed this coast while Mackenzie was travelling across the mountains of B.C. On the shore here, at Sir Alexander Mackenzie Provincial Park, is a rock on which the overland explorer scribed his famous message: "Alex Mackenzie, from Canada, by land, the twenty-second of July, One thousand, seven hundred and ninety-three."

When waters are calm, the area defines fiord. Steep, heavily forested mountain slopes, with rugged peaks mirrored in the turquoise-tinged waters. Plentiful marine life is easy to see in these conditions. Harbour seals, sea lions, orcas, porpoises, eagles, and many varieties of seabirds reveal themselves to the keen observer.

By chartering a boat or float plane from Bella Coola, or paddling to Sir Alexander Mackenzie Park, visitors may see the natural beauty of Dean Channel, and experience a bit of early Canadian history at the same time. Mackenzie and his men spent a night defending the rock, expecting to be attacked by natives hostile towards them earlier in the day. The next day they continued farther along the channel to where Mackenzie could get a reading of his position on the horizon before turning back east.

From Williams Lake take Highway 20 for 466 kilometres to the end at Bella Coola. Boat and float plane tours are available, providing views of Dean Channel on fair-weather days. Boaters' supplies are also available at Bella Coola and there are several campgrounds nearby. Scheduled daily flights serve Bella Coola from Vancouver.

FIORDLAND RECREATION AREA

• **Feature:** Mountains and fiords • **Usual Access:** Remote — boat or float plane • **Time Required:** One week • **Nearest Highway:** Highway 20 • **Best Time To Visit:** June to October • **Charts:** 3738, 3962

THIS AREA of the B.C. coast, northwest of Bella Coola, is deeply incised by long, narrow fiords with forested mountainsides rising almost vertically to the granite peaks of the Coast Range. Waterfalls stream in lacy ribbons, fed by the glaciers above. The sheltered waters here can be glass calm, providing mirror images reminiscent of Norway or New Zealand fiords; or they can be violently whipped into dangerous conditions by winds funnelled down the narrow channels.

This is one of the most difficult parks to reach and even more difficult to explore. A boat or float plane must be used

Granite walls mirrored by the waters of Fiordland Recreation Area.

to get there; the terrain is so rugged that land exploration is extremely limited. Scenic views from the water are so stunning, however, that it is drawing an increasing number of visitors each year, especially those seeking the peace and solitude of remote regions.

Some of the shorelines are suitable for wilderness camping, perfect for ocean paddlers. All visitors should practise good bear-proof camping: this is the domain of the coastal grizzly.

Boats or planes may charter from Bella Coola for sightseeing, or multiday excursions. Some adventure tour operators are considering trips here. For details try the Outdoor Recreation Council of B.C., whose address appears at the back of this book.

Most visitors leave from Bella Coola, a fishing community of 240, reached from Williams Lake by travelling west on Highway 20 for 466 kilometres. The town is also served by scheduled flights from Vancouver.

HAKAI PROVINCIAL RECREATION AREA

• **Feature:** Archipelago • **Usual Access:** Fly-in then kayak
• **Time Required:** One to three weeks • **Nearest Highway:** Highway 20 • **Best Time To Visit:** June to October • **Charts:** 3727 Cape Calvert to Goose Island Including FitzHugh Sound 1:73,600

NAMED AFTER THE HEILTSUK Indian word meaning "wide passage," this offshore archipelago in 1987 became part of the provincial park system. Besides "wide passages" it also features many narrow ones, perfect for ocean kayaking, and a few sandy beaches.

Located east of the Inside Passage, 115 kilometres southwest of Bella Coola, it is extremely remote, accessible only by plane or boat. Like Fiordland, it is a Recreation Area, meaning it is not protected from industrial development. There are several fishing resorts here, taking advantage of the sizable salmon runs through Hakai Pass.

Hakai Recreation Area, encompassing 122,998-hectares,

Hakai Recreation Area, a remote coastal adventure.

is a group of numerous islands, the largest being Hunter and Calvert. Having much of the appeal of the Broken Group Islands of Pacific Rim National Park, it is less crowded with more freedom in choosing secluded campsites. Like the Broken Group, there are sheltered waters suitable for the average paddler, as well as more challenging areas requiring high levels of experience and skill, especially along the exposed western edge of the Recreation Area.

Shorelines vary from sand, shell, and boulder beaches, to exposed rocky headlands. While much of Calvert Island is forested, there are also miles of views of surrounding islands. Long sandy, surf-battered beaches on the west coast of Calvert Island, are reached by a short trail from Kwakshua Channel, between Calvert and Hecate Islands. Delights such as humpback whales in Fitz Hugh Sound, and Steller's sea lions hauling out at Pearl Rocks off the southwest coast of Calvert Island enrich the paddling experience.

MOUNT WADDINGTON

- **Feature:** Highest mountain entirely within B.C. • **Usual Access:** Distant roadside views, charter air flights • **Time Required:** Two days from Williams Lake • **Nearest Highway:** Highway 20 • **Best Time To Visit:** Year round

MOUNT WADDINGTON, at 4,016 metres, is the highest mountain entirely within British Columbia. Considered by climbers as one of North America's finest challenges, it stands in the Coast Mountains of mainland B.C., 155 kilometres due north of the Vancouver Island city of Campbell River. Only forty kilometres from the head of Knight Inlet, Mount Waddington is one in a cluster of peaks higher than three thousand metres. With such high elevation and heavy snowfall, it's winter up here much of the year.

Though Mount Waddington is a well-known feature to northern Vancouver Islanders, there are places throughout the Chilcotin, such as the Tatlayoko-Chilko Lake Road, where the glistening white summit can be clearly seen from a distance. One of the best views, showing the size of the peak compared to those which surround it, is from the trail to the Rainbows, in Tweedsmuir Provincial Park (see the description of the Rainbow Range). A two-hour hike takes you to a plateau with sweeping views of the Coast Mountains to the south, with Mount Waddington standing above all the other peaks.

The best views are from the air. Some pilots will land on the glaciers flowing from the great massif itself. Charters are available from Tatla Lake. Helicopter tours are also available from Chilko Lake Lodge.

BLACKWATER RIVER CANYON

- **Feature:** Rapids, falls • **Usual Access:** Rough road then day hike • **Time Required:** Day trip from Quesnel • **Nearest Highway:** Highway 97 • **Best Time To Visit:** Late April to late October • **Maps:** B.C. Forest Service Recreation Sites - Prince George West

THE CLEAR, DARK WATERS of the Blackwater River flow from the western reaches of the Fraser Plateau to their confluence with the muddy Fraser River, north of Quesnel. In a final rush before losing its identity to the Fraser, the Blackwater flows through Blackwater Canyon. This narrow defile causes the confined river to display a brief fury of white water, a section avoided by even the best canoeists. The river may be explored safely, however, by land on an easy walking trail. It follows the canyon rim through pleasant forests of lodgepole pine and carpets of blue lupines. From either Prince George or Quesnel, this makes a comfortable one-day outing.

Usual access to the trail head is from either Quesnel or Prince George on good gravel roads. From Quesnel, on Highway 97, take the Blackwater Road for sixty kilometres west to the Blackwater River bridge. A B.C. Forest Service campsite just north of the bridge is situated in a shady treed area next to the river. There is no fee for camping here and facilities are basic. Approaching from Prince George, travel south on the Berman Lake Road to the turnoff to Baldy Hughes. Turn south, continuing beyond the end of the pavement at Baldy Hughes, to the Blackwater River bridge.

The three-kilometre trail, sketchy in places, leads from the east end of the forestry campsite downstream on the north rim of the canyon. Hikers should be especially careful near the edges, as they may be undercut, and collapse under a person's weight.

ALEXANDER MACKENZIE HERITAGE TRAIL

• **Feature:** Historic 420-kilometre route • **Usual Access:** Backpacking, horseback, driving, charters • **Time Required:** Three weeks for entire route • **Nearest Highway:** Highway 20 • **Best Time To Visit:** June to September • **Maps:** Strip maps in the book *"In the Steps of Alexander Mackenzie"*; B.C. Forest Service Recreation Sites - Cariboo Region

IN JULY OF 1793 Alexander Mackenzie completed his historic overland journey by canoe and backpack from the eastern side of the Rockies to the Pacific Ocean, becoming the first European to cross the entire continent. His route from the Fraser River west is known now as the Alexander Mackenzie Heritage Trail. It begins near Quesnel where the Blackwater River flows into the Fraser. It is here that Mackenzie, fearing reports of the Fraser's awesome rapids downstream, left his canoes and began the overland journey to the Pacific. The route ends 420 kilometres to the west, at "Mackenzie's Rock" in Dean Channel, where he and his men spent a fearful night expecting to be killed by Indians.

The trip is most frequently made from east to west. The first 340 kilometres, from the Fraser River to Highway 20, is usually done on horseback, or as a backpacking trip. For the first eighty-two kilometres it crisscrosses and sometimes follows logging roads for short distances. The remainder involves traversing large tracts of wilderness past fish-filled lakes and the magnificently-coloured Rainbow Range, before descending to Highway 20 east of Bella Coola. It may be done as day hikes, four-to-five-day backpacking trips, or a major multi-week expedition. Doing the entire trail as one long trip requires outdoor experience and stamina: strong hikers need about two and a half weeks for the whole trip and should make arrangements with an air charter company to replenish supplies at least once along the route.

The eastern trail head is reached from Quesnel or Prince

George. From Quesnel, on Highway 97, take the Blackwater Road for sixty kilometres to the Blackwater River bridge. Continue north for twenty kilometres on the Blackwater Road beyond Punchaw Lake to the Weldwood Road. Turn east (right) on this road and follow it to its end at kilometre "0" of the Mackenzie Trail. If doing any more than a day hike on the trail it is best to arrange a drop off here, rather than leave a vehicle parked for long periods of time.

From Prince George the trail head is reached by travelling south on the Berman Lake Road to the junction with the road to Baldy Hughes. Turn south on this road and travel beyond the end of the pavement at Baldy Hughes another twenty kilometres to the Weldwood Road that turns off to the east (left). A parking lot for the Mackenzie Trail is at the end of the Weldwood Road.

The eastern section of the trail from kilometre "0" at the Fraser River roughly follows the Blackwater River west past Euchineko Lakes, Kluskus Lakes, Tsacha Lake, Tsetzi Lake to kilometre 222 at Eliguk Lake. Eliguk Lake, where Mackenzie spent the night of July 13, 1793 is a half-hour flight from Nimpo Lake on Highway 20. It's a good place to have supplies flown in or to arrange to be picked up or dropped by float plane.

The western section of the route runs from Eliguk Lake 118 kilometres to Highway 20 via the Dean River, Tanya Lakes, Mackenzie Valley, Rainbow Range, and Tweedsmuir Provincial Park to the end of the trail at Burnt Bridge on Highway 20. This point on the highway is approximately three hundred kilometres west of Williams Lake. From here Highway 20 becomes the route through the scenic Bella Coola Valley to the port of Bella Coola, 466 kilometres west of Williams Lake. A boat is required beyond Bella Coola to reach the official end of the route at Mackenzie's Rock on Dean Channel, in Sir Alexander Mackenzie Provincial Park. Charters are available in Bella Coola.

The excellent trail guide *"In the Steps of Alexander*

Mackenzie" by Hasse Bunnelle and Halle Flygare, suggests the following itinerary of overnight camps on a sixteen-day trip to complete the 258-kilometre backpacking trail. It begins at the Upper Titetown Trail intersection with the Batnuni Haul Road at kilometre eighty-two:

Day 1: Chinee Falls — kilometre 98.5
Day 2: Euchineko Lakes Ranch — kilometre 125
Day 3: Sandyman Crossing — kilometre 135.5
Day 4: Squirrel Lake — kilometre 154
Day 5: Sandy Point (Tsacha Lake) — kilometre 179.8
Day 6: Pan's Fish Camp — kilometre 197
Day 7: Rest Day (Re-supply)
Day 8: Cottonwood Creek — kilometre 210
Day 9: West end Eliguk Lake — kilometre 227
Day 10: Gatcho Lake — kilometre 246
Day 11: Dean River ford — kilometre 262.5
Day 12: Squiness Lake — kilometre 275
Day 13: Tanya Lakes — kilometre 288
Day 14: Rainbow Cabin — kilometre 309
Day 15: Bluff Lake — kilometre 325
Day 16: Highway 20 — kilometre 340

From the Blackwater bridge the trail can be reached at several points. The site of Mackenzie's camp on July 5, 1793 at Cleswuncut Lake now is a B.C. Forest Service campground between Blackwater Crossing and Baldy Hughes. This requires no hiking at all to experience a bit of the original adventure.

The Euchineko River area can be reached from Gillies Crossing where the Nazko Road intersects the Batnuni Haulroad. There are hiking trails here as well as four-wheel-drive and horseback routes along the Mackenzie Trail.

Farther west along Highway 20 there is excellent backpacking from Heckman Pass, leading to the Rainbow Range and Mackenzie Pass area of the trail in just a few hours. (See the Rainbow Range entry).

Burnt Bridge, the western terminus of the hiking trail, has

maintained trails good for day hikes with views of the Bella Coola Valley and the site of Friendly Village, where Mackenzie first met the coastal Indians.

The Alexander Mackenzie Trail Association in Kelowna, has detailed information on the historic trail.

BOWRON LAKE CANOE CIRCUIT

• **Feature:** World-famous canoe route • **Usual Access:** Multiday water trip • **Time Required:** Seven to ten days • **Nearest Highway:** Highway 26 • **Best Time To Visit:** Late May to early October • **Maps:** NTS 1:50,000 93H/02,03,06; BC Parks brochure - Bowron Lake

WILDERNESS ADVENTURERS from all over the world travel to Bowron Lake Provincial Park to tour the famous paddlers' circuit. Along the 117-kilometre loop paddlers traverse nine lakes, and portage a total of nearly ten kilometres. The circuit is usually paddled in a clockwise direction, the direction of the current for most of the trip. Chances of seeing

Wilderness paddling at Bowron Lake.

Chances of seeing wildlife are excellent, especially during early mornings. Moose, deer, black and grizzly bears, beavers, and a multitude of bird species including bald eagles may be seen during the seven to ten days it usually takes to complete the trip. Quiet paddlers can often get good animal photographs with a telephoto lens.

The trip begins from the park headquarters, a two-hour drive east of Quesnel. To get there turn east off Highway 97 onto Highway 26, five kilometres north of Quesnel. Drive Highway 26 east for eighty-six kilometres to Bowron Lake Road, which turns north off Highway 26, six kilometres east of Wells. Bowron Lake Park headquarters are reached from this turnoff by travelling the gravel road for twenty-three kilometres north.

All paddlers must register and pay at the park headquarters before setting out. Special permission is required in advance for groups of more than six people, otherwise it is on a first-come-first-served basis. Before leaving the parking lot ensure your vehicles and valuables are secure.

The trip begins with a challenge — a portage to Kibbee Lake, a distance of 2.4 kilometres. The trail is well maintained, and canoe racks for resting are provided at intervals along the trail. Some paddlers use collapsible dollies for portages, especially convenient as most portages are planked boardwalks.

Launch canoes and kayaks at Kibbee Creek, the outlet of Kibbee Lake, and location of a beaver dam where beavers can often be spotted. This initial paddle is only 2.4 kilometres to a campsite, and the second portage, at the east end of Kibbee Lake.

The two kilometre portage trail leads to a campsite at Indianpoint Lake. Along the 6.4-kilometre north shore of this lake are several more campsites including a group campsite. Near a cabin at the northeast end, a small marshy area marks the start of a 1.6-kilometre portage to Isaac Lake. Watch for moose and waterfowl near this marshy area, especially

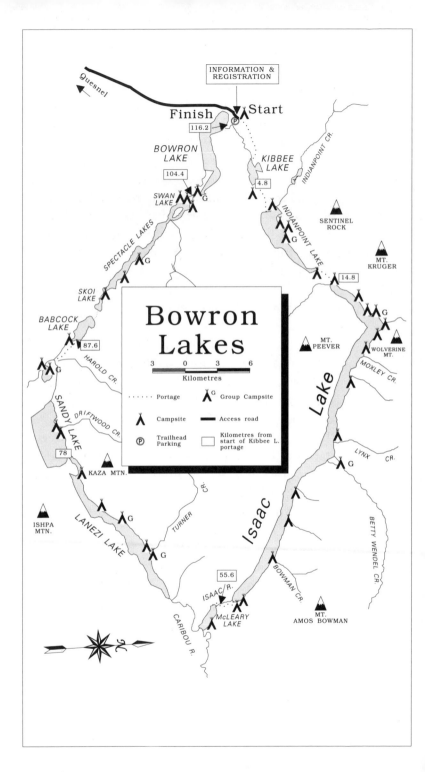

at sunrise or dusk.

Isaac Lake is large, thirty-eight kilometres long and paddlers should be wary of weather: storms develop quickly. Paddling south on Isaac Lake you will pass Mount Peever, Ford Peak, and Mount Faulkner. All campsites along this lake are on the north and west shores.

At the end of Isaac Lake paddlers have the option of a 2.8-kilometre portage to McLeary Lake campsites, or if experienced, and having reconnoitered the chute of the Isaac River, may choose to paddle four hundred-metres of the upper section of the Isaac River, ending at the large, clear pool before Isaac Falls. Then you carry your gear past the falls, which shortens the portage by 1.6 kilometres. Dolly Varden, kokanee, and rainbow trout offer good fishing in the Isaac River.

At the end of the 1.2-kilometre-long McLeary Lake the chilly, glacier-fed 5.2-kilometre Cariboo River, an excellent place to spot beaver, leads to Lanezi Lake. This is a challenge for novices, depending on water levels. Wear your lifejacket. At the end of the river before entering Lanezi Lake watch for moose.

Storms rise quickly on Lanezi Lake's 14.8-kilometre length, so stay near the north shore for quick access to campsites. Paddling Lanezi Lake is not recommended if winds are up, due to the lack of landing sites on the shore. The north shore of the lake rises steeply to Needle Point Ridge. The silty waters of Lanezi Lake although beautiful can conceal underwater obstacles, such as rocks, shallows, and deadheads. Be especially aware at the west end as it narrows just before reaching Sandy Lake.

Lanezi Lake flows into Sandy Lake, a leisurely 4.8-kilometre paddle. The waterway narrows, passing the BC Parks patrol cabin at Babcock Creek, (another good place for spotting beavers) where boats can be paddled, pushed, and pulled, up to Babcock Lake.

A four-hundred-metre portage at the far end of

2.8-kilometre-long Babcock Lake, leads to tiny Skoi Lake. Another four-hundred-metre portage leads to the more substantial Spectacle Lakes. Swimming is more feasible in Spectacle and the remaining lakes, as you are now out of the glacial fed waters. Fishing improves as well once out of the glacial fed waters, with Dolly Varden and Rocky Mountain white fish. Pavich Island separates these lakes from Swan Lake.

After leaving Swan Lake keep to the west side where a short stream leads to the Bowron River, an easy paddle for four kilometres to Bowron Lake. The Bowron River, running through marshlands, is a good place to see moose. The upper Bowron River has a sockeye salmon run in August and September, attracting grizzlies to the area.

At Bowron Lake, with its summer cottages and power boats, the wilderness aura dwindles. The final 7.2-kilometre paddle down this lake ends at a government wharf, a few minutes' portage to the campground and parking lot. Bowron Lake has a kokanee salmon run early in the summer.

There are huge clearcuts now in view all along the route. There is a proposed park extension to connect Bowron Lake Park with Wells Gray Park to the southeast, preserving the Betty Wendle Forest, the last untouched forest in the area. This will provide much needed protection for crucial grizzly bear and caribou habitat. There are, however, plans to build a logging road into the area, and begin logging in 1992.

Although a wilderness area, solitude is rare at the height of summer. The circuit is a great meeting place for outdoors lovers from around the world to swap stories while sipping coffee around a campfire. Crowded conditions are minimized somewhat by the registration process. Many paddlers prefer doing this trip in September when insects are fewer, crowds have diminished, and leaves are changing colour.

This is a trip for the fit and experienced, regardless of age, though novices accompanied by experienced paddlers can handle it. Practice trips beforehand will make the journey safer and more enjoyable. Some adventure tour operators offer this as a guided trip for those not wishing to paddle the circuit on their own. Contact Tourism B.C. for more information on tours.

Even though you're not alone remember this is a wilderness area without services of any kind. Self-sufficiency means having necessary equipment for both day use and emergencies. There are no stores, phones or ambulances close-by.

All campsites have setups for hanging food as black bears, in particular, are common along all the lakes. Bring the bug dope, and be bear aware.

FARWELL CANYON

• **Feature:** Canyon and river • **Usual Access:** Roadside • **Time Required:** Half day from Williams Lake • **Nearest Highway:** Highway 20 • **Best Time To Visit:** May to October • **Maps:** B.C. Forest Service Recreation Sites - Cariboo

THE CHILCOTIN RIVER rushes from the melting glaciers of the Coast Mountains towards the Fraser. During this journey it gouges out Farwell Canyon in the sandy soil of B.C.'s Chilcotin country, an hour-and-a-half drive from Williams Lake. This spot is accessible by passenger vehicles, although the gravel road may be dusty on dry summer days. Watch out for logging trucks, and when sightseeing pull as far off to the side as possible, remembering that sandy soil on the shoulders can swallow tires.

From Williams Lake take Highway 20 west for forty-nine kilometres to Farwell Canyon Road. Turn south and go forty-five kilometres. The two bridge crossings are good vantage points over the canyon. Watch for small bands of California bighorn sheep.

Perhaps the best way to see Farwell Canyon is on a

white-water rafting adventure down the Chilcotin River. The Chilcotin is becoming known as one of the best rafting rivers in the province and outfitters are trying to meet the growing demand.

Sitka spruce in the city of Kitimat.

North by Northwest

*E*ncompassing 317,000 square kilometres and stretching across one third of the province, North by Northwest is B.C.'s largest tourist region. Three large provincial parks offer some protection for some of the last remaining true wilderness of North America. Spatzizi Plateau Wilderness Park, Mount Edziza Provincial Park, and Atlin Provincial Park all offer fine scenery and opportunities for viewing and photographing wildlife. The Queen Charlottes, offshore islands significant for diverse and unique lifeforms, lie off the mainland in the Pacific. A national park in the South Moresby area of the Charlottes was being established as this book was going to press. Also in this region, are the wildest river in North America, Canada's most recent and most spectacular volcanic landscapes, vast areas of tundra, jagged mountain massifs, ninety-kilometre-long beaches, archipelagoes of islets cloaked with ancient forest surrounded by marine waters teeming with life.

Most visitors are motorists using the two major routes. Highway 16, the Yellowhead, traverses the southern portion of this region, running from Tete Jaune Cache west to Prince George and beyond to Prince Rupert. The Queen Charlotte Islands are reached from Prince Rupert by air or, more commonly, a car and passenger ferry to Skidegate where Highway 16 continues north to its end at Masset. The other major route is the Stewart-Cassiar Highway (37), bisecting the region north to south through raw wilderness. It connects Kitimat on the coast with Terrace where it becomes High-

North by Northwest

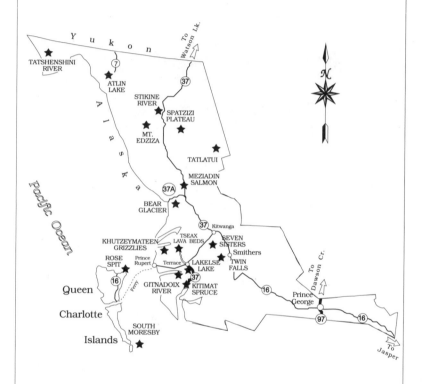

Y u k o n

To Watson Lk.

★ TATSHENSHINI RIVER

⑦ ATLIN LAKE

A l a s k a

Pacific Ocean

STIKINE RIVER

③⑦

★ SPATZIZI PLATEAU

★ MT. EDZIZA

★ TATLATUI

MEZIADIN SALMON

③⑦A

★ BEAR GLACIER

③⑦ Kitwanga

KHUTZEYMATEEN GRIZZLIES

TSEAX LAVA BEDS ★

★ SEVEN SISTERS

○ Smithers

ROSE SPIT ★

Prince Rupert

Terrace

LAKELSE LAKE ★

TWIN FALLS

⑯

Ferry

GITNADOIX RIVER ★

③⑦

★ KITIMAT SPRUCE

⑯

To Dawson Cr.

Queen

Charlotte

Islands

★ SOUTH MORESBY

Prince George

⑯

⑨⑦

⑯

To Jasper

N

Vancouver

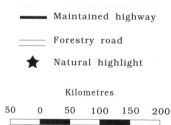

━━━ Maintained highway

──── Forestry road

★ Natural highlight

Kilometres

| 50 | 0 | 50 | 100 | 150 | 200 |

| 30 | 0 | 30 | 60 | 90 | 120 |

Miles

way 16 for a few kilometres until, at Kitwanga Junction, it leaves the main route heading north and once again becomes Highway 37. It is largely gravel but well maintained, a popular alternative route to the Yukon and Alaska as it connects the Alaska Highway with Highway 16.

The main cities of the region are Prince Rupert and Prince George, both served daily by scheduled air and bus services. Sandspit, on the Queen Charlottes, also has daily scheduled flights from Vancouver. Prince Rupert is a busy port with travellers arriving by ferries from Alaska or via the B.C. Ferries Inside Passage route from Port Hardy. The Queen Charlottes are reached from Prince Rupert aboard a six-hour car and passenger ferry that sails to Skidegate.

Physically, North by Northwest is a region of elevated plateaus in the east, separated from the Pacific Ocean by the high glaciated summits of the Coast Range. As with many of B.C.'s regions, the climate varies with distance from coastal areas. Some of the highest rainfall in Canada falls on the coast, yet it is dry in the northeast. Take along wet-weather gear, warm sweaters, and good hiking boots. Again, sunscreen and insect repellent are high on the list.

Long hours of summer daylight (up to nineteen hours in the north) make long, spectacular sunsets, especially after storms when clouds are breaking up. North by Northwest often takes first-time visitors by surprise, with its large number of natural attractions and tantalizing areas of wilderness.

SMITHERS TWIN FALLS

• **Feature:** Waterfalls in a scenic amphitheatre • **Usual Access:** Short walk • **Time Required:** One hour from Smithers • **Nearest Highway:** Yellowhead Highway (16) • **Best Time To Visit:** May to October • **Maps:** BC Forestry Services Recreation Sites - Smithers & Hazelton Area

A WELL-KEPT SECRET in the Smithers area is Twin Falls. Hudson Bay Mountain, a massive, snow-covered summit reaching 2,621 metres toward the sky, dominates the views south of town. A closer approach reveals a magnificent pair of waterfalls, each more than 150 metres high, tumbling into opposite corners of a natural amphitheatre. These falls, fed by Kathlyn Glacier, are not within a park or reserve and are not well known: it's not unusual to have them to yourself.

From Smithers these falls can be seen on a whirlwind one-hour tour. From the Smithers Travel Infocentre take Yellow-head Highway (16) west for 3.6 kilometres, turn left onto Beach Road, and continue 1.2 kilometres to Lake Kathlyn Road. Follow Lake Kathlyn Road, and at 1.1 kilometres turn left onto Glacier Gulch Road. Drive 3.9 kilometres to a B.C. Forest Service recreation site where there is parking. Four-wheel-drive vehicles may go another two hundred metres closer to the falls. From the end of the road a four-hundred-metre path leads up to the base of the falls on the left, offering views of both cascades. One hundred metres before the falls is a platform offering views of both left and right cascades.

The water from both falls feeds a rushing stream in a gully filled with dense slide alder. This thicket provides habitat for a variety of birds. In spring it is a good place to see warblers, vireos, and flycatchers.

The B.C. Forest Service recreation site has tables, and is a relaxing place for a picnic with views of the falls just a few steps away.

SEVEN SISTERS

• **Feature:** Mountain peaks • **Usual Access:** Roadside • **Time Required:** One and a half hours from New Hazelton • **Nearest Highway:** Yellowhead Highway (16) • **Best Time To Visit:** May to October • **Maps:** NTS 1:50,000 103I/16

Seven Sisters Peaks between Prince George and Prince Rupert.

THE MOUNTAIN MASSIF called Seven Sisters is one of B.C.'s most spectacular sets of peaks viewable from a paved road. Their high altitude and ragged appearance is reminiscent of the Ten Peaks rising above Moraine Lake in the Rockies near Lake Louise. Rising suddenly along the road to Prince Rupert, they stand against the dark green of evergreen forests and local farmlands. The highest peak of the group is Mount Weeskinisht, nearly twenty-eight hundred metres. The north side of the massif, heavily cloaked in glacial ice, is especially impressive in early morning or at sundown as the ice turns pink against the violet hues of the cliffs.

Travel west on Yellowhead Highway (16) from New Hazelton for 46.5 kilometres to views of the peaks. The chain of peaks to the south, with a serrated top, is the Seven Sisters Group.

TSEAX LAVA BEDS

• **Feature:** Recently-formed lava • **Usual Access:** Roadside

- **Time Required:** Day trip from Terrace • **Nearest Highway:** Yellowhead Highway (16) • **Best Time To Visit:** May to September • **Maps:** NTS 1:50,000 103P/02,03; BC Forest Service Recreation Sites - Smithers and Hazelton Area

THE MOST RECENT lava flows in Canada are found in British Columbia's Wells Gray Provincial Park. Just about as recent, and far more accessible to the average traveller, are the Tseax Lava Beds north of Terrace.

The lava covers thirty-nine square kilometres and features lava tube caves, vertical shafts where trees were surrounded by flowing molten rock, and cinder cones. It presents a scene of devastation. And so it was, when the lavas flowed from Aiyansh volcano in the mid-seventeen hundreds. An estimated two thousand people perished.

Now the area is receiving some protection as the proposed Nisga'a Memorial Provincial Park. Trails have not yet been developed, so visitors must make their own hiking routes across the rough lava surface. There are no campsites in the immediate area but several are available in Terrace.

To reach the Tseax Lava Beds travel three kilometres west of Terrace on Yellowhead Highway (16) and turn north on Kalum Road. This is an active logging road so exercise caution during the week. It is eighty kilometres to the Nass-Tseax Lava Beds.

LAKELSE LAKE

- **Feature:** Scenic lake, old growth forest • **Usual Access:** Roadside • **Time Required:** Half day from Kitimat or Terrace • **Nearest Highway:** Stewart-Cassiar Highway (37) • **Best Time To Visit:** May to October • **Maps:** BC Parks Brochure - Lakelse

THIS LAKE and surrounding area are known for great fishing, birding, and as home of a white phase of the black bear known as the Kermode. At two separate locations the area is protected as Lakelse Lake Provincial Park. Within these boundaries are beautiful stands of old-growth Sitka Spruce forest with short trails winding through giant trees and lush ferns. The lake, part of the Skeena River system, is a major producer of salmon. Trumpeter swans winter here and eagles, ospreys, and owls are common. More than one hundred bird species have been recorded around the lake. In August, Williams Creek attracts hundreds of visitors who come to see the sockeye spawn.

To reach the park areas at Gruchy's Beach and Furlong Bay, take the Stewart-Cassiar Highway (37) south for twenty kilometres towards Kitimat from the junction of Stewart-Cassiar and Yellowhead Highway (16).

The salmon-viewing area is reached by a one-kilometre trail to Gruchy's Beach. Through a cool forest of large trees and small clearings, keen observers find a variety of plants, including chocolate lilies, Solomon's seal, and twisted stalk. This is also black bear habitat, so make some noise when travelling this trail in spring to avoid surprising a bear.

The section of Lakelse Lake Park at Furlong Bay has a good campsite with showers. Trails loop from the campground through old-growth forests. Pileated woodpeckers, great horned owls, and saw-whet owls are just a few of the interesting forest birds commonly seen or heard.

KITIMAT SPRUCE

- **Feature:** Giant Sitka spruce • **Usual Access:** Roadside
- **Time Required:** One hour from Kitimat • **Nearest Highway:** Yellowhead Highway (16) • **Best Time To Visit:** Year round

COLLECTORS OF BIGGEST, highest, deepest, or oldest can find a natural attraction in the smelter town of Kitimat, on B.C.'s northwest coast. The oldest known spruce tree in the province is safely standing in a small park within Kitimat's city limits. While shorter than many of the giant sitka spruce of Vancouver Island's Carmanah and Walbran valleys, this ancient spruce is 50.3 metres high, 11.2 metres around, and 3.35 metres in diameter. It contains enough wood to frame nine average-sized houses. (Why do we always tend to measure big trees by how much lumber they'd provide if we cut them down?)

To get to Kitimat from Prince Rupert take Yellowhead Highway (16) east for 140 kilometres to Terrace, then take the Stewart-Cassiar Highway (37) south for fifty-seven kilometres to Kitimat. This giant spruce tree is in Radley Municipal Park on Dike Road. Take Haisla Street to Kuldo Avenue, go left for one block to Columbia, right for four blocks to the dike, then right on gravel, taking the first left for three hundred metres to the parking lot. There are several large spruce trees in the park, but the largest is fifty metres straight ahead from the park entrance.

GITNADOIX RIVER

• **Feature:** Wilderness river area • **Usual Access:** Boat across Skeena River • **Time Required:** Day trip • **Nearest Highway:** Yellowhead Highway (16) • **Best Time To Visit:** May to October • **Maps:** NTS 1:50,000 103I/03,06

THE GITNADOIX is a pristine river on B.C.'s northwest coast, draining an area of 58,000 square kilometres. A tributary of the Skeena, Gitnadoix is the Tsimshian Indian word for "people of the swift water." This untouched watershed has numerous geothermal springs, major salmon runs, and enormous potential for wilderness recreation. Mountain goats, grizzly and black bears, trumpeter swans, even harbour seals a hundred kilometres from saltwater are found here.

This special area, accessible by boat, is particularly appealing to white-water paddlers who kayak or canoe the lower reaches of the river.

Travel via Yellowhead Highway (16) for fifty kilometres west of Terrace to Exchamsiks Provincial Park. The Skeena River must be crossed here to reach the Gitnadoix, which is almost directly opposite the park. There is overnight camping in the park.

KHUTZEYMATEEN GRIZZLIES

• **Feature:** Grizzly bears • **Usual Access:** Remote water access — charters available • **Time Required:** Four-day charters from Prince Rupert • **Nearest Highway:** Highway 16 • **Best Time To Visit:** June to September • **Maps:** NTS 1:50,000 103I/12

THE KHUTZEYMATEEN, a remote wilderness in northwest B.C., is one of the few coastal watersheds that supports a significant grizzly population — about fifty bears. Once widespread, the grizzly bear is suffering now from severe habitat reduction. Away from the coast, only a few isolated pockets of habitat remain, mainly in the Rockies and interior mountain ranges. While the coast of B.C., like Alaska and the Yukon, has healthy populations, grizzlies nonetheless are threatened by the industries of people. Logging the old forests causes erosion and silting of streambeds, which damages spawning areas for salmon, an important part of a grizzly's diet. While grizzlies can survive in second-growth forests, they fare better on the nutritious understory of mature, untouched forests.

Environmentalists are lobbying to have the Khutzeymateen preserved as a 39,000-hectare grizzly sanctuary. As a result it is currently the focus of several studies. Conser-

Khutzeymateen Valley, home of the grizzly.

vation groups are sponsoring research to determine which stands of timber should be saved if a battle over use of the area develops. Other work is being done on behalf of loggers to determine the economic feasibility of logging the giant old-growth spruce in the valley. Its remoteness, north of Prince Rupert, makes access difficult for both visitors and loggers: perhaps this will help save it.

There is no easy access to this area. Only boats, float planes, or helicopters can get here. The best, and safest way to visit and see the bears is with an outdoor travel guide, or an organized group led by experienced guides. Remember that despite efforts on their behalf, these are still grizzlies, dangerous and unpredictable. A knowledgeable guide can increase the safety margin immensely. Some tour operators now are regularly visiting the valley as interest increases through public awareness. Contact Travel Infocentres.

ROSE SPIT—EAST SIDE BEACH WALK

- **Feature:** Wild beach • **Usual Access:** Day hike, backpack
- **Time Required:** One to eight days • **Nearest Highway:**
Yellowhead Highway (16) • **Best Time To Visit:** Year round
- **Maps:** BC Parks brochure - Naikoon

THE QUEEN CHARLOTTE ISLANDS are recognized world-
wide for their biological diversity and appealing scenery. The
largest of the 150-odd islands in the group is Graham Island, with a five-kilometre-long taper of sand culminating
in Rose Spit, at the northeast end. Rose Spit separates Dix-
on Entrance from Hecate Strait. Waves from these waters
collide here, tossing sand, driftwood, and shells onto the
narrow spit.

The turbulent waters produce a rich food supply, attracting a great variety of birds, especially during spring and fall
migrations. Sandhill cranes nest in the boggy areas of the
72,641-hectare Naikoon Provincial Park, which encompasses ninety-four kilometres of sandy shore along the western
edge of Hecate Strait. Whales — grays and orcas — are often
seen from the spit. This is an area of such biological importance that it is designated as an ecological reserve. This official status prohibits hunting, camping, fishing, use of
motorized vehicles or any other activity which disturbs the
natural surroundings.

It is a popular place to spend a day, hiking to the tip of
the spit at Rose Point or exploring the dunes and beach areas.
An excellent place to view the spit from a high vantage point
is Tow Hill, a half-hour hike, ending at the top of a one-
hundred-metre-high basalt formation.

B.C. Ferries from Prince Rupert dock at the Skidegate terminal, on Graham Island. Drive north from Skidegate on
Highway 16 for forty-two kilometres to the parking lot at
the Agate Beach Campground. The hike to Tow Hill takes
about one half hour return. There are views out to the end

of the spit and, on extremely clear days, to the snow-capped peaks of Alaska.

The short way to the end of the spit is a beach walk from the campground at Agate Beach. This takes two to three hours, depending on how often you stop to look for shells, jellyfish, and other pelagic treasures. Take some fresh water, sunscreen, wind-waterproof clothing, and tide tables for Prince Rupert.

The long way to the point is to backpack the ninety-four-kilometre East Beach from Tlell. This ranks as one of the longest wilderness beach hikes in the world and takes four to six days to complete.

Harsh prevailing winds blow from south to north, the recommended direction for hiking the beach, keeping the wind at your back. Begin at Tlell by taking a four-kilometre trail along the north side of the Tlell River to the beach, then hiking 4.5 kilometres to the Mayer River crossing. All rivers along the route are wadeable at low tide. The wreckage between the Tlell River mouth and the Mayer River is from the vessel *Pesuta* that washed up in 1928. There is camping at the Mayer River, a good choice for the first night.

It is six kilometres from Mayer River to Cape Ball River, kilometre 14.5 in the trip and another fine camping spot. BC Parks recommends that hikers leave Cape Ball River on a receding tide to avoid being trapped at the base of cliffs along the route.

From Cape Ball River it is sixteen kilometres north to the next camping spot, and 36.5 kilometres to the next major crossing at Oeanda River. Along the way are good campsites at Eagle, Frenchman, and Mortell creeks. The water in these coastal creeks is often brownish but is potable after boiling.

Seventeen kilometres north of Oeanda River is the Cape Fife trail head, sixty-five kilometres from Tlell. From here hikers can take the shorter route by cutting off onto the Cape Fife Trail to Tow Hill, or continuing along the beach to the base of Rose Spit and walking along North Beach to Tow Hill. The cutoff option makes the entire hike from Tlell to Tow Hill seventy-eight kilometres; keeping to the beach makes a total of eighty-nine kilometres. The tip of Rose Spit is another five kilometres.

Hikers who prefer a lighter taste of these sweeping beaches can take a three-day, thirty-one-kilometre hike from Tow Hill. Walk the Cape Fife Trail ten kilometres to East Beach. From here hike twenty-one kilometres along the beach, cutting off at the base of Rose Spit back to Tow Hill.

SOUTH MORESBY

• **Feature:** Misty islands and marine life • **Usual Access:** Remote — boat charters available • **Time Required:** One week • **Nearest Highway:** Yellowhead Highway (16) • **Best Time To Visit:** June to October • **Charts:** 3808 Juan Perez Sound 1:37,500; 3809 Carpenter Bay to Burnaby Island 1:37,500; 3825 Cape St. James to Houston Stewart Channel 1:40,000; 3853 Cape St. James to Cumshewa Inlet and Tasu Sound 1:150,000

THE QUEEN CHARLOTTES, known as the Misty Isles, are often enshrouded in mist, making them hauntingly beautiful. To the natives they are "Haida Gwaii" — islands of the people. Moresby, the most southerly of the two main islands, is called "Gwaii Hanaas," meaning islands of wonder and beauty. Deeply indented with inlets and bays, with scores of islands and islets offshore, the southern portion of Moresby Island is designated now as Gwaii Haanas-South Moresby National Park Reserve. Towering spruce forests with hanging lichens and ankle-deep carpets of moss are inhabited by plants and animals found nowhere else. The surrounding waters teem with rich marine life from starfish and shellfish to orcas and gray whales, sea lions, and porpoises.

South Moresby is a special place, significant not only provincially, but internationally.

The Queen Charlottes may be reached by car-and-passenger ferry from Prince Rupert, and by scheduled air service from Vancouver or Prince Rupert. Paved roads are few, and although logging roads seem to be everywhere, they do not provide good access to the most special areas.

Ocean kayakers by the hundreds explore the waters of South Moresby each year. Some travel on their own; others take commercial sailing or kayaking tours. Whatever the preference, visitors should make arrangements well in advance and try not to be constrained by a rigid timetable. Things often move slowly in the Charlottes.

A boat or air-charter tour is also a good way to see South Moresby. Visitors who have not made arrangements before coming to the Queen Charlottes can charter locally in Queen Charlotte City and get permission for visiting Indian villages from the Skidegate Band council office. Kayaks and adventure-tour packages may be arranged in Queen Charlotte City.

The operative word for weather in these Misty Isles is wet. More than two hundred days each year have some precipitation, with October claiming the distinction of being the wettest month, averaging more than 201 millimetres of rain. Rain in the peak tourist season — May to August — is usually in the range of fifty-eight millimetres, with temperatures around 17 degrees Celsius. Even on days that don't receive measurable amounts of rain you can still get damp from fog and sea spray: good waterproof clothing is a must. Properly equipped, visitors here enjoy the magic of South Moresby even without the postcard-type sunny days.

MEZIADIN SALMON RUN

- **Feature:** Salmon spawning • **Usual Access:** Roadside
- **Time Required:** Day trip from New Hazelton • **Nearest**

Highway: Stewart-Cassiar Highway (37) • **Best Time To Visit:** August to October

FROM EARLY AUGUST until early October, sockeye salmon arrive at the fish ladders on the Nass River to spawn. Although not as large as the famous Adams River runs, the sockeye runs here are significant. More than a quarter of a million fish return, providing an awesome natural spectacle, especially in peak years. The brilliantly-coloured fish fight the current of the Nass River, having travelled fifty-kilometres from the Pacific Ocean. A visit to view this natural wonder makes a pleasant stop on the Stewart-Cassiar Highway, or a day outing from New Hazelton on the Yellowhead Highway.

Meziadin Junction is near the south end of the Stewart-Cassiar. From the junction of the Yellowhead and the Stewart-Cassiar travel north on the Stewart-Cassiar for 145 kilometres to the Nass River bridge. Three hundred metres north of the bridge is a turnoff west to the viewing area.

There is camping nearby at Meziadin Lake Provincial Park, fourteen kilometres north of the Nass bridge.

BEAR GLACIER

• **Feature:** B.C.'s only roadside glacier • **Usual Access:** Roadside views • **Time Required:** One hour from Meziadin Junction • **Nearest Highway:** Highway 37A • **Best Time To Visit:** May to October

BEAR GLACIER, the only roadside glacier in the province, is a half-hour drive west of the Stewart-Cassiar Highway near Meziadin Junction. Motorists can marvel at the aqua hues of the ice in the glacier's snout. You may even see gigantic blocks of ice crash to the outwash plain at its base. When water levels are low, you can walk closer to the glacier's face:

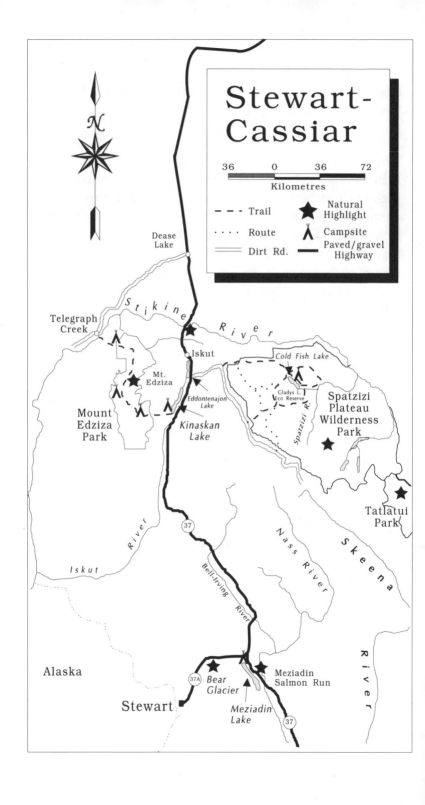

the more wading you're prepared to do, the closer you can get.

This is a short side trip for those travelling the Stewart-Cassiar Highway. It is twenty-five kilometres west of Meziadin Junction, 158 kilometres north of the Yellowhead Highway. The highway travels through Bear Pass where there are distant views of the glacier. The best views, however, are close up, from the roadside lower down the valley towards the coast. The glacier almost reaches the road from the south side.

Weather in this area is often cloudy and cool, even in summer, because of the proximity to the Pacific Ocean and the effects of the Coast Range. Even on the common dull days, however, the glacier is impressive and the colours of the ice often seem even better when the sun is not shining. Keep a lookout for the abundant, but hard-to-spot wildlife of the area. Grizzlies often feed on salmon in the rivers, deer and moose browse in the valleys, and mountain goats balance precariously on the cliffsides. A variety of hardy wildflowers manages to grow in the gravel adjacent to the river flowing from the glacier's snout.

If you decide to approach the glacier, don't get too close to the broken snout. Calving ice blocks, hundreds of kilos each, give no warning.

Even viewed from a distance, the intensity of the blue hues inside the crevasses is remarkable, varying from translucent aqua near the surface to a rich cobalt deeper in the ice mass. High snowfalls in the Coast Mountains, have compressed over thousands of years into extremely dense ice, resulting in the rich hues. Throughout the Coast Range these rivers of ice creep down the slopes, filling most of the higher-elevation valleys. In the past they extended into the river valleys through which many roads now travel, including Highway 37A. Today most of the glaciers have retreated and require rigorous hikes or mountaineering skill to get close views. Bear Glacier is the exception, as it is only a hundred metres from the highway.

TATLATUI

- **Feature:** Wilderness area • **Usual Access:** Remote fly-in
- **Time Required:** One week from Prince George • **Nearest Highway:** Stewart-Cassiar Highway (37) • **Best Time To Visit:** June to September • **Maps:** NTS 1:50,000 94D/13

TATLATUI PROVINCIAL PARK is a 105,826-hectare wilderness on the border of Spatzizi Provincial Park. It is located along the western fringes of the Skeena Mountains, about two hundred kilometres due north of New Hazelton. Visitors usually fly into Tatlatui's larger lakes and explore the area on their own, using topographical maps. Others take guided horseback trips.

Most of the park lies above eleven thousand metres. It features large expanses of treeless meadows and rocky summits, the highest being the 2,350-metre Melanistic Peak. There are several lakes in the area: the largest are Kitchener and Tatlatui. Large animals such as grizzlies, black bears, caribou, and mountain goats roam these hills. Because of the remoteness and lack of developed trails it is best to join a guided tour for a first-time trip here.

MOUNT EDZIZA

- **Feature:** Shield volcano • **Usual Access:** Fly-in • **Time Required:** Flightseeing or one week • **Nearest Highway:** Stewart-Cassiar Highway (37) • **Best Time To Visit:** June to September • **Maps:** NTS 1:50,000 104G/07

MOUNT EDZIZA, at 2,787 metres, is the focal point of one of the most stunning volcanic areas in Canada. It is preserved as part of the 230,000-hectare Mount Edziza Provincial Park and Recreation Area, along with multihued volcanic mountains and features with tantalizing names like Cocoa Crater, Spectrum Range, and Coffee Crater.

This remote area is about 340 kilometres north of Prince Rupert. Visitors should be guided, or be hardy and experienced wilderness travellers. At higher elevations especially, where the terrain is treeless, there are unlimited backpacking possibilities. Point-to-point multiday hikes are possible by getting dropped by float plane and arranging a pickup a few days later. Several air operations in the Iskut area offer this service. During an overland trek there are good chances to see black and grizzly bears, Stone sheep, Osborne caribou, moose, and even wolves.

If a multiday fly-in backpacking trip isn't possible, then a one-to-two-hour flightseeing tour is a good alternative. The landscape of brightly streaked cones and craters is actually more formidable in its barrenness, when seen from the air.

Volcanic activity as recent as thirteen hundred years ago has resulted in features like Eve Cone, Coffee and Cocoa Craters. Coloured from browns to magentas to bone white, their slopes are still relatively naked as plant communities have not had time to gain a foothold.

Travelling into the area on foot is possible, but a boat is required to reach the trail heads. Trails are not maintained and considerable effort and time are needed to reach the more easily-travelled high areas. This makes the fly-in option appealing, especially for second-time visitors who may feel they wasted valuable days on their first trip bushwacking up to the highlights.

To reach the Mount Edziza area travel north from the junction of Yellowhead Highway and the Stewart-Cassiar Highway. About 370 kilometres north of the junction there is camping at Kinaskan Lake Provincial Park, and one of the trails into Mount Edziza begins here. At Iskut, forty kilometres farther north on the Stewart-Cassiar, visitors can arrange for guides or get information about trail conditions and access.

Telegraph Creek, a major embarkation point to the park, is west of Dease Lake, which is 492 kilometres north of the

Yellowhead and Stewart-Cassiar junction. At Dease Lake check with the provincial highways office about road conditions to Telegraph Creek. If the report is good, leave RVs and trailers behind and travel the Telegraph Creek Road west over 119 kilometres of winding, narrow, gravel with huge dropoffs just inches from your tires. If your stomach can take it, it's well worth the trip just for the tremendous views of the Stikine River.

Self-guiding parties have a choice of three routes into the Mount Edziza Park. The Mowdade Trail begins across from Kinaskan Lake Provincial Park, forty kilometres south of Iskut on the Stewart-Cassiar. This route runs twenty kilometres to the Coffee and Cocoa Craters area south of Mount Edziza. The second route is into Buckley Lake via the Klastline River Trail, which starts at the A-E Guest Ranch in Iskut. But there isn't a bridge across the Klastline River to the trail head, so arrangements to get across must be made. The third access is from the community of Telegraph Creek, 119 kilometres west of Dease Lake at the end of the exciting cliffside road. This trail to Buckley Lake begins across the Stikine River: for a small fee you can be ferried across by a local resident. These options are for the seasoned backpacker who doesn't mind spending time following old trails before getting to the really scenic delights of Mount Edziza.

Most people prefer to fly into one of the beautiful lakes close to the craters, either Mowdade or Buckley. From either of these lakes options exist for day hikes and overnight backpacking trips in the vicinity of Mount Edziza and the craters surrounding it. There is also a five-to-seven-day route connecting Mowdade and Buckley lakes. Flights may be arranged in Dease Lake, Eddontenojon Lake, or Telegraph Creek.

Guides are available for hiking trips and horseback excursions into the park. These may be arranged at Iskut, Eddontenojon, Telegraph Creek, and Dease Lake.

Spatzizi Plateau. (Gail Ross photo)

SPATZIZI PLATEAU

• **Feature:** Alpine tundra plateau • **Usual Access:** Backpack or fly-in • **Time Required:** One week • **Nearest Highway:** Stewart-Cassiar Highway (37) • **Best Time To Visit:** June to September • **Maps:** NTS 1:50,000 94E/04; BC Parks brochure - Spatzizi; Canoe Sport BC - British Columbia Canoe Routes

SPATZIZI PLATEAU WILDERNESS Provincial Park, a total of 675,000 hectares, is B.C.'s second-largest provincial park. About three hundred kilometres north of Smithers, it encompasses parts of the Skeena Mountains and Spatzizi Plateau. This enormous outback is connected to a number of other wilderness areas — the 217,000-hectare Stikine River Recreational Area on the north and west; the 230,000-hectare Mount Edziza Park and Recreation Area to the west; and the 105,826-hectare Tatlatui Provincial Park to the southeast. In all, these continuous wilderness areas encompass more than 1.2 million hectares, some 233,580 hectares more than Tweedsmuir, B.C.'s largest provincial park.

Miles of rounded summits and tundralike plateaus are ideal for extensive backpacking and day hikes from nearby base camps. More than a dozen small lakes dot the landscape and two major rivers flow through the park. The treeless terrain of higher elevations makes wildlife viewing easy. Most visitors fly into a base camp at Coldfish Lake and explore from there.

Spatzizi is east of the Stewart-Cassiar Highway communities of Iskut and Dease Lake. There is four-wheel-drive access to the park boundary. Take the Stewart-Cassiar north from Kitwanga for 361 kilometres to Tatogga Lake. Follow the Ealue Lake Road east for twenty-two kilometres to the Klappon River crossing and the B.C. Rail grade. This becomes a very narrow road from which two trails lead into the park.

The first trail head along the B.C. Rail grade is the beginning of the McEwen Creek route to Coldfish Lake. This route is also a horse trail and may be quite mushy in areas. It is about thirty-five kilometres to Coldfish Lake Camp. Another hiking route is from a marked trail-head sign along the B.C. Rail grade indicating the route up Eaglesnest Creek. This is about forty kilometres, skirting the Gladys Lake Ecological Reserve before reaching Coldfish Lake.

Although some people hike into the park from these road accesses, most prefer to fly in by charter float plane from Dease Lake, Eddontenojon Lake, Terrace, or Smithers, usually to Coldfish Lake. It is the site of an old hunting camp and seven cabins are available for use by the public for up to seven days at a time.

Flightseeing tours also can be arranged. There are camp-sites at Eddontenojon Lake and Kinaskan Provincial Park, and more civilized shelter at private lodges outside the park boundaries.

Named for the Tahltan Indian word meaning "red goat" after the goats' habit of rolling in the reddish soils of the area, Spatzizi Provincial Wilderness Park surrounds the 48,560-hectare Gladys Lake Ecological Reserve, an area of total protection for Stone sheep and mountain goats. There is no camping or any other activities that disturb the natural state of the area. Day trips are permitted into the Ecological Reserve, which is just south of Coldfish Lake Camp.

The Spatzizi Plateau contains the headwaters of the Stikine River, one of the last great wild rivers of North America. There is a popular 260-kilometre canoe route from Tuaton Lake down the Stikine to a pullout on the Stewart-Cassiar just upstream from the impassable Grand Canyon of the Stikine. Paddlers and canoes are flown in by float plane to Tuaton Lake or Laslui Lake. Dangerous rapids, about 1.5 kilometres below Laslui Lake, and five hundred metres beyond Chapea Creek, require major portages totalling six kilometres. Depending on water levels, more portages may be required around dangerous rapids. This trip is recommended only for advanced wilderness canoeists. Guided trips may be arranged.

A less-demanding river trip, but still recommended for advanced canoeists, is the Spatzizi River. There are no major rapids: the only difficult section, at Beggarly Creek Canyon, can be bypassed on a bridge. The Spatzizi trip is extremely scenic and best done in late August and September. The foliage turns wonderful shades of rust, yellow, and crimson late in the season.

There is a price to pay here for the relatively inexpensive access. Canoes and gear must be portaged the first five kilometres from the parking lot.

STIKINE RIVER

• **Feature:** Wild river • **Usual Access:** Views from roadside
• **Time Required:** Full day drive from New Hazelton
• **Nearest Highway:** Stewart-Cassiar Highway (37) • **Best Time To Visit:** May to September • **Maps:** NTS 1:50,000 94E/04; BC Parks brochure - Spatzizi; Canoe Sport BC - British Columbia Canoe Routes

THE STIKINE, a Tlingit Indian word meaning "the river," is one of the great rivers of North America and, unfortunately, one of the last running wild and free. The Stikine begins at Tuaton Lake in Spatzizi Plateau Wilderness Park, and runs a total of 460 kilometres to the Alaskan coast near Wrangell. It contains a significant physical feature of international stature. The narrow gorge called the Grand Canyon of the Stikine, is a ninety-six-kilometre stretch where the river squeezes between rock walls up to three hundred metres high. This furious section has yet to be paddled successfully. Mountain goats are often seen on the near-vertical walls of the canyon; other big game animals such as grizzly bears and caribou live in the hills of the surrounding plateau. It is easy to get a good look at this mighty river as the Stewart-Cassiar Highway crosses it just south of Dease Lake.

The Stikine River bridge, upstream from the Grand Canyon, is the easiest place to view the river. These upstream waters are calmer, flowing from their source in Spatzizi Plateau Provincial Park.

The Stikine bridge is reached by travelling the Stewart-Cassiar Highway north for 443 kilometres from the Yellowhead Highway junction at Kitwanga. The bridge is thirty-two kilometres north of Iskut. Travellers heading south on the Stewart-Cassiar reach the bridge about 280 kilometres south of the Alaska Highway.

Canoeists and rafters can travel 260 kilometres from Tuaton Lake down the Stikine to the pullout at Highway 37 before the Grand Canyon. There are several difficult portages between the launching point and the pullout at the Stikine River bridge. Paddlers and canoes are flown in by floatplane to Tuaton Lake or Laslui Lake. Dangerous rapids, about 1.5 kilometres below Laslui Lake, require a 1.2-kilometre portage. Five hundred metres beyond Chapea Creek there's another major portage. Depending on water levels, more portages may be required around dangerous rapids.

Canoes and gear require ground transportation to bypass the Grand Canyon section, between the Stikine Bridge and Telegraph Creek. At Telegraph Creek the river trip can be resumed to its end at Wrangell, Alaska, where air charters must be arranged. It is possible to arrange for a jet boat pickup from the river mouth for a return to Telegraph Creek.

A trip on the Stikine must be well planned. It is remote: even minor mishaps can become tragic in such an isolated wilderness. This is considered a wild river as no roads come within three hundred kilometres of its mouth.

ATLIN LAKE

• **Feature:** Lake and mountain scenery • **Usual Access:** Roadside • **Time Required:** Two to seven days from Whitehorse • **Nearest Highway:** Alaska Highway • **Best Time To Visit:** June to August • **Maps:** NTS 1:50,000 104N/04,05,12,13; 104M/01,08

ATLIN LAKE, a total of 744 square kilometres, is the largest natural lake in British Columbia. Located in the extreme northwestern corner of the province, it lies between the Tagish Highlands and the high glaciated summits of the Coast Mountains. Silty meltwaters feeding the lake from the glaciers to the west, give it a beautiful greenish-blue hue. The Llewellen Glacier, a massive ice sheet covering more than 70,000 hectares south of the lake, dominates the terrain

Llewelyn Glacier above Atlin Lake. (Gail Ross photo)

and attracts climbers from around the world.

Only the northeastern part of the lake is accessible by road, the rest is raw wilderness. Most of the southern lakeshore and surrounding area are part of Atlin Provincial Park, a vast wilderness where only the self-sufficient should venture. Wildlife viewing is excellent: black and grizzly bears, caribou, moose, lynx, wolves, and B.C.'s only herd of Dall sheep. Scenic Atlin Lake rightly deserves its nickname, "The Switzerland of the North."

The lake is reached by taking the Alaska Highway to Jake's Corner, sixty-five kilometres south of Whitehorse, or 369 kilometres north of Watson Lake. Highway 7, a good gravel road connects Jake's Corner with Atlin, ninety-eight kilometres to the south. A scenic drive, the road travels beside

Little Atlin Lake, then Atlin Lake itself, with sweeping views of the Coast Mountains to the west.

Atlin Provincial Park and Recreation Area, encompasses 271,140 hectares of lake and surrounding mountains from Theresa Island southwest of Atlin, to the Alaska border. Travellers must be well equipped and experienced, as this area has no services.

Travel to the lake's most interesting wilderness areas in the park is usually by power boat or canoe. People without boats can arrange in Atlin for guides, float plane trips, and air sightseeing charters.

There are few established hiking trails but you can scramble up many of the lakeshore mountains to the alpine without too much bush thrashing. Only skilled, roped mountaineers should venture onto the glaciers.

Take heed of the lake's Indian name, "aht-lah." It means "big" or "stormy water." Storms come howling across the Coast Mountains without much warning and quickly whip the calm surface of the lake into whitecaps, endangering small craft.

Camping is primitive here, wherever you find a good spot. From virtually any lakeshore camp there is great scenery and excellent opportunities for meals of fresh grayling and char.

TATSHENSHINI RIVER

• **Feature:** Wildest of North American rivers • **Usual Access:** Rafting or kayaking • **Time Required:** One day to three weeks • **Nearest Highway:** Haines Highway • **Best Time To Visit:** June to September • **Maps:** NTS 1:50,000 114P/05,06,11,14; 115A/02,03

TAKE NOTE of the name "Tatshenshini." It is certain to be a resounding battlecry for wilderness lovers in the nineties. The Tatshenshini, the wildest of North American rivers, is threatened by a proposed copper mine.

The "Tat" rises in extreme northwestern B.C., raging north into the Yukon before winding back into B.C. again, finally merging with the Alsek River before emptying into the Pacific Ocean through Alaska. Both the Alaskan and Yukon governments have protected their sections of the river by granting it park status. British Columbia has not.

The Tat is significant in myriad ways. It passes the world's largest non-polar icefield on its 256-kilometre run from its headwaters west of the Haines Road, near the Yukon border in northwestern B.C. A major salmon run occurs in this river yearly. A rare blue variation of a black bear, known as the glacier bear, is found only here. Significant populations of grizzlies and wolves, decimated elsewhere, still exist in the area. Dall sheep, moose, martens, beavers, ermines, foxes, you name it — all are found in a pristine river valley. The conditions are so untouched that the Tat has been referred to as an "Ice Age River." Its turbulent waters are significant on the scale of the Colorado, which is the only North American river more threatened than the Tatshenshini. On another list, the Tat is considered to be in the top three white-water rafting rivers in the world. All these things must surely add up to more value than one copper mine.

The recommended way to see the Tat is on guided white-water rafting parties. First run successfully in 1976, it is a serious undertaking, not for open canoes paddled even by experts. This river is for extremely skillful white-water kayakers.

From Whitehorse, Yukon, travel the Alaska Highway to Haines Junction, then take the Haines Highway south. The launching point is at an abandoned settlement, Dalton Post, reached by a dirt road leaving the west side of the Haines Highway between Pringle and Stella lakes. Although the river may be run in three to five days, the best trips are about ten days, taking time to relax and explore the valley, to enjoy the camaraderie that grows on a wilderness trip. You can fly out of Dry Bay, Alaska, at the end of the journey.

Kinuseo Falls in Monkman Park.

Peace River-Alaska Highway

T he remote Peace River-Alaska Highway region encompasses the entire northeast quarter of B.C. Its vast wilderness and isolation attract the most self-sufficient travellers, lured by the waterfalls, natural hot springs, hot swamps, and wildlife.

The main route through this region is Highway 97 from Prince George to Dawson Creek. From Dawson Creek the Alaska Highway continues northwest across the entire region into the Yukon Territory near Watson Lake. This drive offers the best opportunities in North America to see big-game animals in their natural habitat. Even motorists will likely see moose and Stone sheep, maybe porcupines and black bears. Those venturing away from the Alaska Highway have a better chance of seeing species such as grizzlies, goats, wolves, and wolverines.

The Alaska Highway is no longer an epic gravel journey of broken windshields and flat tires. These things do occur, but most of the road between Dawson Creek and White-horse now is paved. Distances between services are greater than in most other areas of the province, however, so motorists should make sure they fill up with fuel long before the tank is empty. Visitors travelling this region have usually arrived from southern B.C., or have come through the Inside Passage on car ferries, then through Alaska and the Yukon on the Alaska Highway. The other main road to the area is Highway 2 from Edmonton, Alberta, via Grande Prairie.

Peace River-
Alaska Highway

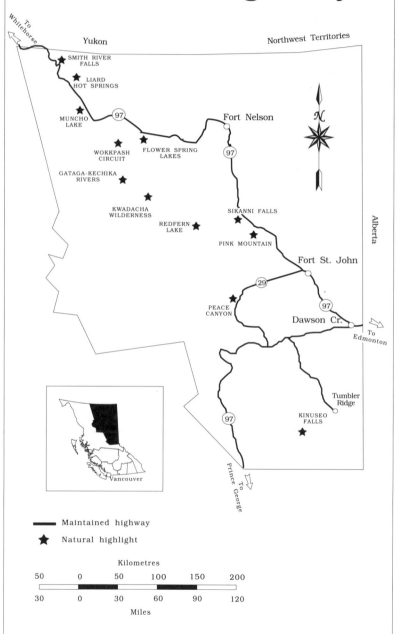

To Whitehorse

Yukon

Northwest Territories

SMITH RIVER FALLS

LIARD HOT SPRINGS

MUNCHO LAKE

97

Fort Nelson

WOKKPASH CIRCUIT

FLOWER SPRING LAKES

97

GATAGA-KECHIKA RIVERS

KWADACHA WILDERNESS

REDFERN LAKE

SIKANNI FALLS

PINK MOUNTAIN

Fort St. John

29

Alberta

PEACE CANYON

97

Dawson Cr.

To Edmonton

Tumbler Ridge

KINUSEO FALLS

97

Vancouver

To Prince George

—— Maintained highway

★ Natural highlight

Kilometres

| 50 | 0 | 50 | 100 | 150 | 200 |

| 30 | 0 | 30 | 60 | 90 | 120 |

Miles

This region is unique in that it contains the only part of B.C. which lies east of the Rocky Mountains. The great backbone of North America, the Rockies gradually become lower and more rounded before finally petering out in the northern part of this region near Muncho Lake. To the east is a vast tract of foothills and prairies. To the west of the Rockies lie remote, game-rich valleys and the terminus of the sixteen hundred-kilometre gash in the earth known as the Rocky Mountain Trench. This region contains the headwaters of the Peace River, the only river cutting through the Rockies from east to west, on its way towards the Arctic Ocean. This is the only region in B.C. where virtually all the rivers drain into the Arctic Ocean rather than the Pacific Ocean.

There are several beautiful provincial parks and recreation areas. Three provincial parks — Stone Mountain, Muncho Lake, and Liard River Hot Springs — are on the Alaska Highway and have good camping facilities. Wokkpash Recreation Area features a strenuous wilderness backpacking loop through Canada's best example of hoodoo formations. Kwadacha Wilderness is usually reached by float plane and offer adventure for experienced, hardy wilderness travellers in areas of high game concentrations.

Short, dry summers and long, cold winters characterize this region. Summer temperatures are usually lower than those elsewhere and to say the weather is unpredictable is an understatement. Southeastern winds can bring extreme hot or cold weather. Brief rain showers are not uncommon and evenings are always cool. It is advisable to carry wet-weather gear, comfortable clothing, sturdy shoes, insect repellent, and long-sleeved shirts when walking in the bush. Snow is possible at all times of the year, especially at higher elevations.

The remoteness and rugged terrain on explorations away from the roads require parties to be fit, experienced, and well equipped for multiday treks. Long days of early summer, this being the north, allow for more progress than in areas farther south, and the extended dusk hours make wild-life sightings more common. The hot springs along the Alaska Highway make for a pleasant respite after a tough backpacking or canoe trip, so bring a bathing suit. Some of the small lakes are usually warm enough for swimming in summer.

PEACE CANYON

• **Feature:** River gorge • **Usual Access:** Roadside • **Time Required:** Two hours from Fort St. John • **Nearest Highway:** Highway 29 • **Best Time To Visit:** High water - spring and early summer • **Maps:** Outdoor Recreation Council - #16 Peace River-Liard Region 1:250,000

THE PEACE RIVER has been tamed by dams, but the canyon carved over thousands of years by roaring white waters is still impressive. During times when the water volume released by the dam is high, the river and canyon regain some of their former magnificence. In 1793 this stretch of river was so treacherous that it almost finished off explorer Alexander Mackenzie and his men before forcing a major portage. The canyon is near the town of Hudson's Hope, between Fort St. John and Chetwynd, and can be seen from the highway.

To reach the Peace River Canyon take Highway 97 twelve kilometres north from Fort St. John. Turn south on Highway 29 and travel seventy-five kilometres to Hudson's Hope and beyond eight kilometres to the Peace River bridge.

KINUSEO FALLS

• **Feature:** Wilderness waterfall • **Usual Access:** Remote fly-in or jetboat • **Time Required:** One to seven days from Dawson Creek • **Nearest Highway:** Highway 29 • **Best**

Time To Visit: June to September • **Maps:** NTS 1:50,000 93I/11; Outdoor Recreation Council - #16 Peace River-Liard Region 1:250,000; BC Parks brochure - Monkman

KINUSEO FALLS are the highest of many waterfalls to be found in the remote wilderness of Monkman Provincial Park. A large emerald-green pool lies at the base of the sixty-nine-metre cascade, a good place to catch arctic grayling. Perhaps this contributed to their Indian name, meaning "fish." The falls are on the Murray River, in the Hart Ranges of the northern Rockies east of the Rocky Mountain Trench. Charter jetboats take day trips along the Murray River to the base of the falls from Tumbler Ridge. An exciting, but sometimes frustrating alternative is to drive the washed out four-wheel-drive dirt road that leads into the area from Tumbler Ridge.

Access to this area is usually by float plane, landing at one of the many small lakes then hiking to the falls. There are wilderness campsites and three waterfall-viewing areas in Monkman Park. Trails are being upgraded. Contact BC Parks in Fort St. John for an up-to-the-minute report on conditions and routes. This is a wilderness area so all travellers must be self sufficient.

A rough twenty-two-kilometre trail from Kinuseo Falls to Monkman Lake runs through beautiful subalpine lake country. This is high country, where grizzlies may be encountered: hang your food; cook away from tents.

PINK MOUNTAIN

• **Feature:** Wildflowers, especially fireweed • **Usual Access:** Roadside • **Time Required:** Day trip from Fort St. John • **Nearest Highway:** Alaska Highway • **Best Time To Visit:** June to August • **Maps:** NTS 1:50,000 94G/02; Outdoor Recreation Council - #16 Peace River-Liard Region 1:250,000

PINK MOUNTAIN is a rounded summit with such a profusion of fireweed covering its slopes that it appears pink from a distance. It can be seen from the Alaska Highway, 162 kilometres north of Fort St. John, or from a forestry road leading to its summit. The expanse of fireweed in summer provides an awesome panorama from the top, looking out over the low, forested hills of the Peace River country beyond to the peaks at the very end of the northern Rockies.

You may see woodland caribou, particularly in fall, and grizzly, bison, whitetail deer, and moose.

From Fort St. John travel north on the Alaska Highway for 160 kilometres, then turn south (left) onto a dirt road which leads three kilometres to the summit, at 1,784 metres.

This alpine area is accessible with a high clearance vehicle in dry weather. Check at the Pink Mountain service station before setting out in a two-wheel-drive vehicle.

REDFERN LAKE

• **Feature:** Alpine lake • **Usual Access:** Remote fly-in • **Time Required:** One week • **Nearest Highway:** Alaska Highway • **Best Time To Visit:** July to September • **Maps:** NTS 1:50,000 94G/05 East & West; Outdoor Recreation Council - #16 Peace River-Liard Region 1:250,000

REDFERN LAKE is another of those tiny turquoise mountain lakes that can only be described as a jewel. It lies south of the Alaska Highway, northwest of Pink Mountain, west of the Rocky Mountain Trench. It is surrounded by glaciated summits. Several other pretty lakes in the area may be reached by foot from Redfern. Fairy, Trimble, and College lakes all have stunning alpine scenery. Big game abounds in this area, accessible by foot, horseback, or float plane. There are other nearby lakes, waterfalls and alpine tundra

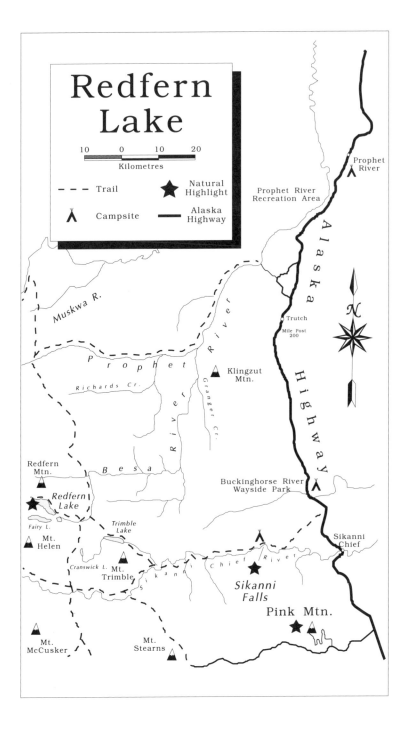

Redfern
Lake

10   0   10   20
Kilometres

- - - Trail

⋀ Campsite

★ Natural Highlight

▬▬ Alaska Highway

Prophet River Recreation Area

Prophet River

Alaska Highway

Trutch

Mile Post 200

Muskwa R.

Prophet River

Richards Cr.

Granger Cr.

Klingzut Mtn.

Besa River

Redfern Mtn.

Redfern Lake

Fairy L.

Mt. Helen

Trimble Lake

Cranswick L.

Mt. Trimble

Buckinghorse River Wayside Park

Sikanni Chief River

Sikanni Chief

Sikanni Falls

Pink Mtn.

Mt. McCusker

Mt. Stearns

to visit as day trips from a base at Redfern Lake. It is currently being considered as a provincial park.

Flying in from Fort St. John is the preferred mode of access but it is possible to reach Redfern on foot or horseback by taking an outfitter's trail from the Alaska Highway, up the Sikanni Chief River to Trimble Lake, then crossing over to the Besa River and on to Redfern.

SIKANNI FALLS

• **Feature:** Waterfall • **Usual Access:** Day hike • **Time Required:** Day trip from Fort St. John • **Nearest Highway:** Alaska Highway • **Best Time To Visit:** June to September • **Maps:** Outdoor Recreation Council - #16 Peace River-Liard Region 1:250,000

SIKANNI FALLS are a seldom seen, picturesque waterfall in northeast B.C., just a two-hour drive north of Fort St. John. A huge gorge lies at the base of the falls where the Sikanni River plunges over a fault in the riverbed. A ten-minute drive from the Alaska Highway, followed by a fifteen-minute hike to a B.C. Forest Service picnic site above the gorge, is a worthwhile price to pay for a view of these falls.

From Fort St. John travel north on the Alaska Highway to kilometre 262, just north of the Sikanni Chief River. Turn south and take the left fork, following the forestry signs to the trail head. The trail meanders gently downhill through aspen forest and ends at the brink of a gorge. There are views of the falls across the gorge. Beware of the edge: it may be crumbly or slippery in wet weather. Don't try to reach the river, as tempting as the emerald pools may be.

During periods of high water, jetboats can make it to the falls on the Sikanni Chief River. Visitors may be able to charter one locally.

GATAGA-KECHIKA RIVERS

- **Feature:** Wilderness float trip • **Usual Access:** Remote
- **Time Required:** Two weeks • **Nearest Highway:** Alaska
Highway • **Best Time To Visit:** August to September
- **Maps:** NTS 1:50,000 94F/13; 94K/04,05; 94L/07,08,10,11,14;
94M/03,04,05,11,12; Outdoor Recreation Council - #16 Peace
River-Liard Region 1:250,000; Canoe Sport BC - British
Columbia Canoe Routes

THE GATAGA RIVER flows west out of the Muskwa
Ranges of the northern Rockies. Summits are lower, gentler than in the south. Float trips through this magnificent
wilderness take from one to two weeks, depending on where
you begin and how much time you spend exploring.

Most people fly out of Fort Nelson. To get to Fort Nelson
travel north on the Alaska Highway to milepost three
hundred, which is five hundred kilometres north of Dawson
Creek. Most travellers then fly to South Gataga Lakes, about
two hundred kilometres southwest of Fort Nelson, or get
dropped on the river forty kilometres downstream from the
lakes. The river travels 320 kilometres through rich game
country, ending at milepost 543 of the Alaska Highway. Paddlers encounter several sets of rapids and about eight
kilometres of nasty portages.

This is a good one-to-two-week wilderness trip by canoe,
kayak, or raft. Caribou, moose, wolves, beavers, grizzly and
black bears may be seen along the way.

KWADACHA WILDERNESS

- **Feature:** Wilderness area • **Usual Access:** Fly-in • **Time
Required:** One to two weeks • **Nearest Highway:** Alaska
Highway • **Best Time To Visit:** July to September • **Maps:**

NTS 1:50,000 94F/10; Outdoor Recreation Council - #16 Peace River-Liard Region 1:250,000

THE KWADACHA is a vast wilderness area of 167,540 hectares at the northern end of the Rocky Mountains. It is a haven for wildlife and outdoors lovers who like to see wolves, elk, grizzly and black bears, Stone sheep, caribou, and moose. There are dramatic rocky summits over 2,500 metres: the highest, Mount Churchill, rises 3,201 metres above sea level. Glaciers hang from the highest peaks. The meltwaters from the most massive, Lloyd George Glacier, become the Kwadacha River, the major waterway of the area.

Since 1973 this has been part of Kwadacha Wilderness Provincial Park. There is one designated trail for multiday treks. The wide alpine valleys and tundra are the setting for expeditions by experienced backpackers or for guided parties on foot or horseback.

Most people fly into the Kwadacha, but there are two guide-outfitter routes to the park open to the public. From Beaver Creek crossing, just north of Trutch on the Alaska Highway, a road goes west to the Prophet River. A 150-kilometre trail beginning just north of Trutch runs up the Prophet to the Muskwa River, then on to Fern Lake just below Bedaux Pass in Kwadacha. Another trail goes from Redfern Lake, via the headwaters of the Besa River, and over to the Prophet where it joins the route described above. Trails here are not maintained and wilderness navigation skills are essential.

Kwadacha is a Sikanni Indian word for "white water," referring to the silty waters of the river. Chesterfield, Haworth, and Quentin lakes, connected by rough trails, are the major lakes of the park. Navigation skills and wilderness expertise are required for a visit here. You may be able to arrange a guided trip to the area. Check with the Travel Infocentre in Fort Nelson for a list of outfitters who may offer this service.

The abundance of rodents in the alpine terrain make the Kwadacha area a good place to see the stately golden eagle, always on the lookout for a meal of Siberian lemming.

FLOWER SPRING LAKES

• **Feature:** Pater Noster lake formation • **Usual Access:** Day hike • **Time Required:** Weekend from Fort Nelson • **Nearest Highway:** Alaska Highway • **Best Time To Visit:** June to September • **Maps:** NTS 1:50,000 94K/07; Outdoor Recreation Council - #16 Peace River-Liard Region 1:250,000

FLOWER SPRING LAKES are fine examples of Pater Noster lakes, arranged steplike in the landscape, resembling prayer beads. Each of the three is dammed by glacial debris, representing major stages in the advances and retreats of local glaciers. Located on the south side of Mount St. George in Stone Mountain Provincial Park, south of the Alaska Highway, they are the source of the North Tetsa River.

These lakes lie in one of the few areas of the province where the alpine tundra is an easy walk from a major highway. Grizzly bears, caribou, and mountain goats can be seen from a distance in the treeless terrain. Ptarmigan cluck and scurry in the rocks around the lakes. Dwarf willow and many specialized tundra flowers, such as woolly lousewort and alpine buttercups, grow along a five-kilometre trail leading to the lakes from the Alaska Highway.

From Fort Nelson on the Alaska Highway travel 123 kilometres north to Summit Lake Campground, in Stone Mountain Provincial Park.

The Flower Spring Lakes trail head is at the Summit Lake Campground, at an elevation of 1,275 metres, the high point of the Alaska Highway. It begins across a footbridge at the south end of Summit Lake, ascending steeply for the first

kilometre through lodgepole pine forest and beds of thick
reindeer moss. After crossing a microwave access road, the
trail slowly gains elevation, running through wide open alpine tundra towards a bowl on the back of Mount St. George.
In fall, the dwarf willow, alpine cranberry, and blueberries
paint the tundra with a mosaic of rusts, scarlets, and yellows. Beyond the lowest lake in the chain the trail becomes
sketchy, but hikers can find the other lakes by following the
stream uphill and ascending terminal moraines that dam
the outlet of each succeeding lake. Views back down the valley towards the Alaska Highway are stunning.

   The elevation and resultant lack of bush makes this area
an excellent place to spend a few days hiking the high open
ridges, perhaps Mount St. George just south of the lake,
or Mount St. Paul, on the north side of the highway.

WOKKPASH GORGE HIKING CIRCUIT

• **Feature:** Wilderness hike • **Usual Access:** Backpack
• **Time Required:** Three to seven days • **Nearest Highway:**
Alaska Highway • **Best Time To Visit:** June to September
• **Maps:** NTS 1:50,000 94K/07,10; Outdoor Recreation Coun-
cil - #16 Peace River-Liard Region 1:250,000

THIS SEVENTY-KILOMETRE JOURNEY is an outstanding
backpacking trip through varying landscapes from alpine
tundra to lakeshores, from river canyons to Canada's most
extensive hoodoos. Hikers share these hills with caribou,
grizzlies, moose, and wolves. It is particularly scenic in fall
when alpine plants turn brilliant crimson and biting bugs
get lazy.

   From Summit Lake in Stone Mountain Provincial Park,
123 kilometres north of Fort Nelson on the Alaska Highway,
go eight kilometres north to Rocky Mountain Lodge and
make arrangements for parking. The trail goes up the Mac-
Donald River from behind the lodge. The trail is not well

Hoodoos at Wokkpash Gorge.

marked and map-reading skill is essential, as well as good preparation for self sufficiency. From the upper MacDonald River the route goes through a pass to the west, passing a few small tundra lakes before turning south before Forlorn Gorge. You can take a detour around Forlorn Gorge through the wonderful game-rich valley immediately east of Whitestone Ridge. An hour or two over easy tundra gets you to the end of the ridge, where a marked trail descends to Plug Creek. From there it follows Plug Creek to Wokkpash Lake. The descent to Wokkpash Lake, and the final thirteen kilometres to the Churchill Mine Road, are especially rugged when conditions are wet.

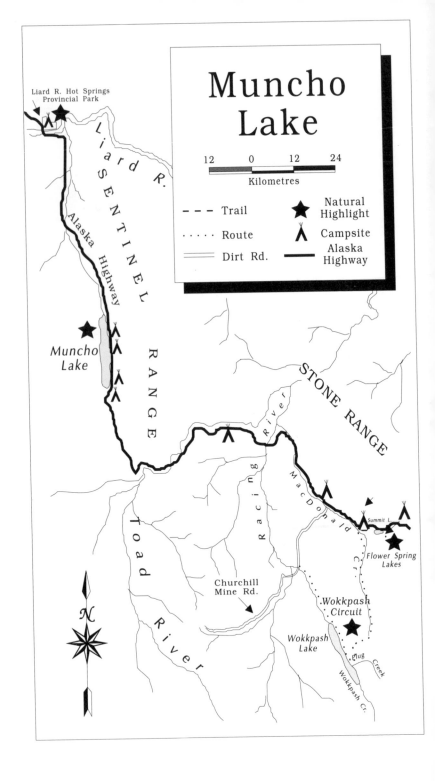

Muncho Lake on the Alaska Highway.

MUNCHO LAKE

• **Feature:** Scenic lake • **Usual Access:** Roadside • **Time Required:** Day trip from Fort Nelson • **Nearest Highway:** Alaska Highway • **Best Time To Visit:** June to September • **Maps:** NTS 1:50,000 94K/13; Outdoor Recreation Council - #16 Peace River-Liard Region 1:250,000

MUNCHO LAKE, meaning "big lake" in local Indian dialect, is the centrepiece of an 88,416-hectare provincial park along the Alaska Highway. It is wonderfully scenic, a narrow, twelve-kilometre-long strip of deep emerald surrounded by the final summits of the Rocky Mountains. It is also the best place in the province for viewing Stone sheep, a species of bighorn that frequents gravelly creeks and mineral licks along the Alaska Highway. Many other large animals — moose, caribou, wolves, coyotes, black and grizzly bears — are often seen during the long twilight hours in early summer. Muncho Lake Provincial Park is 273 kilometres north of Fort Nelson. It is well worth a few days' stop at one of the campgrounds to explore the area.

To reach Muncho Lake travel north on the Alaska Highway for 681 kilometres from Dawson Creek. Exercise special caution while driving the Alaska Highway near the park: Stone sheep are sometimes oblivious to traffic, like some of the tourists watching them.

There is good camping and hiking in the park. Two campgrounds with a total of thirty sites are located on the lakeshore. The gentle surrounding summits offer unlimited day hiking with a minimum of bush thrashing to reach the alpine.

LIARD RIVER HOT SPRINGS

• **Feature:** Hot springs • **Usual Access:** Easy walk • **Time Required:** Weekend from Fort Nelson • **Nearest Highway:** Alaska Highway • **Best Time To Visit:** All year • **Maps:** NTS 1:50,000 94M/08; Outdoor Recreation Council - #16 Peace River-Liard Region 1:250,000

LIARD RIVER HOT SPRINGS are an interesting and relaxing destination on the Alaska Highway in extreme north-central British Columbia. There are several hot pools

Alpha Pool in Liard River Hot Springs Park.

and other natural features associated with the geothermal activity, preserved here in the 668-hectare Liard River Hot Springs Provincial Park. The springs produce a localized warm climate, supporting plant species rarely found this far north — monkey flower, ostrich ferns, and carnivorous sundew, to name a few. The main attractions, however, are two pools suitably warm and clean for soaking — up to 55 degrees Celsius.

The larger spring is Alpha Pool, reached by a boardwalk over a hot swamp. It is the most developed of the pools with change huts and a small rock dam that increases the depth to accommodate large numbers of bathers. Alpha Pool, cooler toward the downstream end, is eighteen metres long. The water enters at 53 degrees Celsius but cools to 42 by the time it reaches the lower end. Beta Pool, above Alpha, is reached by a trail and boardwalk.

From Fort Nelson, at milepost three hundred, take the Alaska Highway north to milepost five hundred and turn right into Liard River Hot Springs Provincial Park. There are fifty-three campsites here, with applicable fees, but no charge for using the springs. From the parking lot there is an easy stroll on boardwalks of about one hundred metres to the main thermal pools.

SMITH RIVER FALLS

• **Feature:** Waterfall • **Usual Access:** Short hike • **Time Required:** Full day from Fort Nelson • **Nearest Highway:** Alaska Highway • **Best Time To Visit:** June to September • **Maps:** Outdoor Recreation Council - #16 Peace River-Liard Region 1:250,000

SMITH RIVER FALLS, like Sikanni Falls, are underrated as a natural highlight. These pretty falls are accessible from the Alaska Highway, twenty-seven kilometres northwest of Liard River Hot Springs. There is good fishing for grayling here and a well-worn trail to the base of the falls through a spruce forest. In autumn there are cranberries, blueberries, and a variety of mushrooms in the mossy forest floor alongside the trail. This is a pleasant diversion from the Alaska Highway.

Useful Addresses

Tourism Associations

For general information or to obtain the free *Accommodations* guide or provincial road maps, write - Tourism BC, 1117 Wharf St., Victoria, B.C., V8W 2Z2.

Tourism Association of Vancouver Island, #302-45 Bastion Square, Victoria, B.C., V8W 1J1.

Tourism Association of Southwestern B.C., Box 48610, Bentall P.O., #101-1425 West Pender St., Vancouver, B.C., V6G 2S3.

Okanagan/Similkameen Tourist Association, #104-515 Highway 97 South, Kelowna, B.C., V1Z 3J2.

Kootenay Country Tourist Association, 610 Railway St., Nelson, B.C., V1L 1H4.

B.C. Rocky Mountain Visitors Association, Box 10, 495 Wallinger Ave., Kimberley, B.C., V1A 2Y5.

High Country Tourist Association, #403-186 Victoria St., Box 962, Kamloops, B.C., V2C 5N4.

Cariboo Tourist Association, Box 4900, 190 Yorston Ave., Williams Lake, B.C., V2G 2V8.

Peace River/Alaska Highway Tourism Association, Box 6850, #10631-100th St., Fort St. John, B.C., V1J 4J3.

North by Northwest Tourism Association, Box 1030, 2840 Alfred Ave., Smithers, B.C., V0J 2N0.

National Parks

Pacific Rim National Park, Box 280, Ucluelet, B.C., V0R 3A0.

Gwaii Haanas/South Moresby National Park Reserve, Box 37, Queen Charlotte City, B.C., V0T 1S0.

Mount Revelstoke National Park, Box 350, Revelstoke, B.C., V0E 2S0.

Glacier National Park, Box 350, Revelstoke, B.C., V0E 2S0.

Yoho National Park, Box 99, Field, B.C., V0A 1G0.

Kootenay National Park, Box 220, Radium Hot Springs, B.C., V0A 1M0.

Provincial Parks

South Coast Region, BC Parks, 1610 Mount Seymour Road, North Vancouver, B.C., V7G 1L3.

Southern Interior Region, BC Parks, 101-1050 West Columbia St., Kamloops, B.C., V2C 1L4.

Northern Region, BC Parks, 1011-4th Ave., Prince George, B.C., V2L 3H9.

Forestry Regions

Vancouver Forest Region, 4595 Canada Way, Burnaby, B.C., V5G 4L9.

Ministry of Forests, 3726 Alfred St., Smithers, B.C., V0J 2N0.

Ministry of Forests, 1011-4th Ave., Prince George, B.C., V2L 3H9.

Ministry of Forests, 515 Columbia St., Kamloops, B.C., V2C 2T7.

Ministry of Forests, 518 Lake St., Nelson, B.C., V1L 4C6.

Ministry of Forests, 540 Borland St., Williams Lake, B.C., V2G 1R8.

Maps

Canada Map Office, 615 Booth St., Ottawa, Ontario, K1A 0E9.

Maps B.C., Parliament Buildings, Victoria, B.C., V8V 1X5.

Geological Survey of Canada, Sales Information Office, 6th floor, 100 West Pender St., Vancouver, B.C., V6B 2R0 (NTS maps).

Outdoor Recreation Council of British Columbia, 1367 West Broadway, Vancouver, B.C., V6H 4A9.

Marine Charts

Department of Fisheries and Oceans, Institute of Ocean Sciences, 9860 West Saanich Road, Box 6000, Sidney, B.C., V8L 4B2.

Most marine stores and the Canadian Hydrographic Service have marine charts and tide tables.

Miscellaneous

Canadian Paraplegic Association, 780 S.W. Marine Drive, Vancouver, B.C., V6P 5Y7.

Western Institute for the Deaf, 2125 W. 7th Ave., Vancouver, B.C., V6K 1X9.

Regional Highlight Guide

VANCOUVER ISLAND

NATURAL HIGHLIGHT	ACCESS	HIGHWAY	PAGE
Botanical Beach	Day hike	4	17
Active Pass	Walk	17/99	19
Englishman River Falls	Walk	4	20
Cathedral Grove	Walk	4	20
Carmanah Valley	Day hike	4	21
Broken Group Islands	Canoe	4	23
West Coast Trail	Backpack	4/14	25
Della Falls	Backpack	4	31
Long Beach	Roadside	4	33
Gray Whale Migration	Boat	4	35
Meares Island	Boat	4	36
Hot Springs Cove	Boat	4	37
Strathcona Meadows	Day hike	4	38
Johnstone Strait Orcas	Boat	19	40
Cape Scott Beaches	Day hike	19	41

SOUTHWESTERN B.C.

Desolation Sound	Boat	101	47
Princess Louisa Inlet	Boat	101	49
Skookumchuck Narrows	Day hike	101	50
Shannon Falls	Walk	99	51
Stawamus Chief	Roadside	99	53
The Black Tusk	Backpack	99	55
Garibaldi Lake	Backpack	99	58
Brandywine Falls	Walk	99	60
Nairn Falls	Walk	99	61
Lizzie-Stein Divide	Backpack	99	61
Meager Creek Hot Springs	Roadside	99	62
Reifel Refuge	Roadside	99	63
Harrison River Eagles	Roadside	7	64
Fraser Canyon	Roadside	1	65
Hope Slide	Roadside	3	67
Sumallo Grove	Roadside	3	67
Blackwall Peak Meadows	Roadside	3	68

OKANAGAN-KOOTENAY

NATURAL HIGHLIGHT	ACCESS	HIGHWAY	PAGE
Yellow Pine Ecol. Res.	Roadside	3	75
Cathedral Lakes	Backpack	3	76
Keremeos Columns	Day hike	3	79
Osoyoos Pocket Desert	Roadside	97	80
Vaseux Lake	Roadside	97	81
Cougar Canyon	Day hike	97	82
Kalamalka Lake	Roadside	97	83
Spectrum Falls	Roadside	6	84
Idaho Peak Meadows	Roadside	31A	84
The Valhallas	Day hike	6	86
Kokanee Glacier	Backpack	3A	87
Kokanee Creek	Walk	3A	89
Kootenay Pass	Roadside	3	90
Creston Valley Wildlife	Roadside	3	93

ROCKY MOUNTAINS

Elk Lakes	Day hike	43	99
Akamina-Kishinena	Day hike	3/93	101
St. Mary's Alpine	Backpack	95A/3A	102
Lussier Hot Springs	Roadside	93	103
Ram Creek Warm Springs	Walk	93/95	105
Dutch Creek Hoodoos	Roadside	93/95	106
Lake of the Hanging Gl.	Day hike	95	107
Cobalt Lake	Day hike	95	109
Columbia Wildlife Area	Roadside	95	111
Wapta Falls	Day hike	1	113
Mount Revelstoke Meadows	Roadside	1	114
Illecillewaet Glacier	Day hike	1	115
Emerald Lake	Roadside	1	116
Lake O'Hara	Backpack	1A	117
Takakkaw Falls	Roadside	1	121
Twin Falls	Day hike	1	123
Sunshine Meadows	Day hike	1	124
Mount Assiniboine	Backpack	1	126

HIGH COUNTRY

NATURAL HIGHLIGHT	ACCESS	HIGHWAY	PAGE
Zopkios Ridge	Roadside	5	133
Adams River Sockeye Run	Walk	1	134
Cache Creek Grasslands	Roadside	1	135
Spahats Creek Falls	Walk	5	136
Trophy Mountains	Day hike	5	137
Dawson Falls	Walk	5	139
Helmcken Falls	Walk	5	141
Murtle Lake	Day hike	5	143
Rearguard Falls	Walk	16	145
Val. of a Thousand Falls	Backpack	16	146
Berg Glacier	Backpack	16	149
Mount Robson	Roadside	16	152
Botanie Valley	Roadside	12	154
Lower Stein Valley	Day hike	12	156

CARIBOO-CHILCOTIN

Alkali Lake	Roadside	20	163
Chilko Lake	Roadside	20	165
Chilanko Marsh	Roadside	20	167
Rainbow Range	Backpack	20	167
Hunlen Falls	Backpack	20	170
Dean Channel	Boat	20	172
Fiordland	Boat	20	173
Hakai Recreation Area	Boat	20	175
Mount Waddington	Roadside	20	177
Blackwater River Canyon	Day hike	97	177
Mackenzie Trail	Backpack	97/20	179
Bowron Lake Circuit	Canoe	26	182
Farwell Canyon	Roadside	20	187

NORTH BY NORTHWEST

NATURAL HIGHLIGHT	ACCESS	HIGHWAY	PAGE
Smithers Twin Falls	Walk	16	193
Seven Sisters	Roadside	16	194
Tseax Lava Beds	Roadside	16	195
Lakelse Lake	Roadside	16	196
Kitimat Spruce	Walk	37	197
Gitnadoix River	Boat	16	198
Khutzeymateen Grizzlies	Boat	16	199
Rose Spit—East Beach	Day hike	16	201
South Moresby	Boat	16	203
Meziadin Salmon Run	Roadside	37	204
Bear Glacier	Roadside	37A	205
Tatlatui	Aircraft	37	208
Mount Edziza	Aircraft	37	208
Spatzizi Plateau	Aircraft	37	211
Stikine River	Roadside	37	214
Atlin Lake	Roadside	7	215
Tatshenshini River	Raft	3(YT)	217

PEACE RIVER-ALASKA HIGHWAY

Peace Canyon	Roadside	29	224
Kinuseo Falls	Aircraft	29	224
Pink Mountain	Roadside	97	225
Redfern Lake	Aircraft	97	226
Sikanni Falls	Day hike	97	228
Gataga-Kechika Rivers	Aircraft	97	229
Kwadacha Wilderness	Aircraft	97	229
Flower Spring Lakes	Day hike	97	231
Wokkpash Gorge	Backpack	97	232
Muncho Lake	Roadside	97	235
Liard River Hot Spr.	Walk	97	236
Smith River Falls	Day hike	97	238

Recommended Reading

Carey, Neil G. *A Guide to the Queen Charlotte Islands, 1989-90.* Anchorage: Alaska Northwest Books, 1989.

Chettleburgh, Peter. *An Explorer's Guide: Marine Parks of British Columbia.* Vancouver: Special Interest Publications, 1985.

Fairley, Bruce. *A Guide to Climbing and Hiking in Southwestern British Columbia.* Vancouver: Gordon Soules Publishing, 1986.

Harris, Bob. *The Best of B.C.'s Hiking Trails.* Surrey: Heritage House/BC Outdoors, 1986.

Jones, Elaine. *The Northern Gulf Islands Explorer—The Outdoor Guide.* Vancouver: Whitecap Books, 1991.

Macaree, Mary and David. *103 Hikes in Southwestern British Columbia.* Vancouver: Douglas & McIntyre, 1987.

Nanton, Isabel and Simpson, Mary. *Adventuring in British Columbia.* Vancouver: Douglas & McIntyre, 1991.

Neave, Roland. *Exploring Wells Gray Park. Third edition.* Kamloops: The Friends of Wells Gray Park, 1988. (Box 1386, Kamloops, B.C. V2C 6L7.)

Obee, Bruce. *The Gulf Islands Explorer—The Outdoor Guide,* 1990. *The Pacific Rim Explorer—The Outdoor Guide.* Vancouver: Whitecap Books, 1986.

Patton, Brian and Robinson, Bart. *The Canadian Rockies Trail Guide—A Hiker's Manual to the National Parks.* Banff: Summerthought, 1989.

Stoltmann, Randy. *A Hiking Guide to the Big Trees of Southwestern British Columbia.* Vancouver: Western Canada Wilderness Committee, 1987.

Woods, John G. *Glacier Country: A Guide to Mount Revelstoke and Glacier National Parks.* Vancouver: Douglas & McIntyre, 1987.

Woodworth, John and Flygare, Halle. *Trail Guide: In the Steps of Alexander Mackenzie.* Toronto: The Nature Conservancy of Canada, 1987.

Wright, Richard T. *The Bowron Lakes-A Year Round Guide.* Surrey: Heritage House, 1985.

INDEX

Maps and photos are in italics; main entry in bold

About the Authors

Steve Short has worked with British Columbia youth since 1971 as an outdoor leader and director of wilderness programs. After leaving college he took up residence in a remote cabin on the Yukon River, where he developed his love for the wilderness. As a professional photographer, mountaineering, backpacking and kayaking are part of his working life. His nature and outdoor photographs are published internationally in calendars, postcards, books, and magazines such as *Canadian Geographic, Beautiful British Columbia, Equinox, Westworld*, and others.

Bernie Palmer was born and raised in the outback of northern B.C. where her father was a guide-outfitter. Nature and the outdoors were a way of life for Bernie, often living in areas accessible only by plane, horseback, or dog sled. Her concern for the environment has grown from her childhood days. She's an avid backpacker, skier, canoeist, and nature photographer.